BLYTH

MEMORIES

Blyth – 1940.

Jim Harland

The chain ferry which plied between North and South Blyth. Named the High Ferry it is known that a rowing boat acted as the link between both sides of the river for over 300 years as the crossing began life as a ford.

Copyright Jim Harland 2010

First published in 2010 by

Summerhill Books
PO Box 1210
Newcastle-upon-Tyne
NE99 4AH

www.summerhillbooks.co.uk

Email: summerhillbooks@yahoo.co.uk

ISBN: 978-1-906721-27-5

Contents

An aerial view of Blyth showing the complete set of windmills along the pier taken in 2006. Missing from the shot are the three larger windmills just off shore which have been plagued by breakdowns since their installation.

4

Introduction

There have been, over the years, a number of very good books on memories of Blyth but this one, I feel, has been waiting to be written for quite a while. While capturing the tales of long ago from some of our contributors I have also concentrated on individuals who have made a contribution to the business, social and industrial life of the town. I have been fascinated to hear some of the previously unheard tales direct from the mouths of those involved.

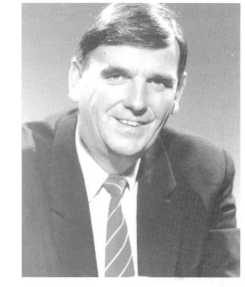

Among those who have opened their secrets to me are Lord Glenamara, the former Ted Short, the visionary headmaster of Princess Louise Road Modern School, now living in a residential home in Hexham; George Watson and Jacky Marks both of Blyth Spartans fame; Don Kent, the former general manager of the Blyth Harbour Commission who lives in retirement in Whitley Bay and Edith Mitcheson, the golfing centenarian and widow of Harry Mitcheson the former head of the Blyth Dry Docks and Shipbuilding Company. To those and all the others featured in this book my grateful thanks.

Incidentally those acquaintances of mine who don't recognise the accompanying picture, I would point out it was taken in 1983 to hang in the foyer of BBC Television Centre in Newcastle where I worked until my retirement as sports and outside broadcast producer. It replaces, at my wife Rosemary's insistence, a picture my publisher preferred of me with a huge boa constrictor around my neck which was taken in the Tiger Balm Gardens, Singapore, on my return from the 1982 Commonwealth Games in Australia.

I hope the tales you are about to read give you different perspective on some of the happenings in my home town of Blyth.

Jim Harland
Blyth, 2010

Acknowledgements

My sincere thanks to Gordon Smith, Blyth's leading historian and Michael Goonan of Scenic Photos for pictures and information, Gerry Evans for his "detective work", the European Library, the Evening Chronicle, News Post Leader, the Blyth Harbour Commission, my wife, Rosemary, for her patience and support and to all who have contributed towards the production of this book.

The junction of Regents Street and Waterloo Road taken in the 1920's. The large building on the left is the Central Methodist Church, in the far distance is the spire of the Presbyterian Church of England later to be converted in Woods Pop Factory.

Bombs Over Blyth
and Newsham

The bombing of Blyth and Newsham in 1940 still lives in the memories of many in the town. Here we read of the experiences of three Blyth citizens when the bombs fell. The first is Alf Douglas who was born in 25 Disraeli Street on August 14th, 1929, the son of Bill and Ethel; next comes Joan Waddle who first saw the light of day at 20 Park Road on May 23rd, 1924, the daughter of Harry and Esther Tweedy, and then Jim Derbyshire who was born on December 3rd, 1934 at 6 Single Row, South Newsham, the son of Jim and Anne, and has spent all his life in the village.

Alf Douglas' Memories:

I can remember when war was declared because the Government had already delivered our Anderson shelter which we were supposed to erect in our garden as far away from the house as possible.

The shelter was a number of corrugated metal sheets which had to be bolted through at the top but first you had to dig a deep trench to give you added protection. My Dad, me and older brother Matt set about it and eventually got it finished and even put in a concrete floor.

My Dad then sent me to Yarrows shop in Disraeli Street, which was run by two sisters, to get some potato sacking bags to use as sand bags on top of the shelter. We had no sand so we filled them with soil.

Everything was completed by the time the first siren sounded. Actually we were in what was called the "Phoney War" with nothing happening for several months but I still grabbed my pet tortoise and my favourite horse-racing game and took them down with us. It was quite cosy as we had a concrete floor and Dad had put in stove fire with the chimney sticking out of the top of the shelter.

When the bombers started to come over my Dad, who was an Air Raid Warden based at the nearby school, would dash over to tell us when a red alert had been sounded meaning Jerries were on the way. We would then head straight into the shelter. The first explosion we heard was when a parachute mine fell about half a mile away on top of the Station Signal Box which was at the end of the platform. The site is now part of the Morrison's car park. We heard later that the signalman had been killed and lines and waggons destroyed. The force of the explosion was such that a waggon wheel was embedded into the Presbyterian Church in Waterloo Road, some 300 yards away, and a heavy rail coupling clamp which kept rails together fell on top of a house, through the roof and the middle of a bed in which three children had been sleeping before the alert and ended up in the kitchen. There was lots of damage to houses in Bondicar Terrace, Maddison Street and Alexandra Crescent, the Redheads sweet factory was also hit. Everyone who was bombed out was taken to the Welfare Hall in Renwick Road where a huge pile of mattresses had been stored on the stage for some time anticipating such an event. Two of the youngsters who had makeshift beds were Gerry Evans, later to become part-time leader of Blyth YMCA, and Frankie Riley, Blyth's answer to Frank Sinatra.

At the time we didn't realise just how much bombing was going on in and around Blyth in 1941. It was only later we learned that twelve people were slightly injured when high explosive bombs were dropped in the area. The police station had windows shattered and there was a lot of damage in the town centre. There were reports of two deaths – one in Catherine Terrace and the other at the Bebside railway crossing while ten people were seriously injured and sixty three slightly.

The German raids though didn't stop us playing out particularly in the tank traps which had been built at the top of Temples field which was named after the local farm. I used to walk to that farm every day from our house in Lilac Avenue to collect a pint of fresh milk in a tin billy can.

Another of my daily jobs was to lift the flooring in the shelter to see if any water had seeped in on the concrete floor. If it had it was up to me to bale it out.

The tank traps we played in were about six to eight feet wide and about six feet deep. They had one straight side and one slanted one. We never did find out if they could stop a tank, thank goodness.

Mind you we always made sure we were at Temples field on a Sunday morning because that was the time the local the Home Guard unit trained.

My brother Matt, although he had no military experience, had been given the rank of major and while he was provided with a suitable military tunic he had, like all the others in the unit, to wear his own trousers. Unlike Dad's Army on the television they had been issued with rifles. I don't know if they had ammunition but they certainly didn't have grenades as during their practises they had to use pieces of rock which caused some accidental damage to one or two volunteers when the throwing went awry.

Matt was working on munitions in Vickers Armstrong in Elswick and had to start early about seven o'clock and in consequence didn't get home till about eight or nine at night. He took to sleeping in the shelter so he could get off quickly for the bus first thing in the morning.

Joan Waddle's Memories:

I was sixteen and working as a shorthand typist in Newcastle when the war come to Blyth. We were still living in Park Road where my mother had made a very comfortable shelter under the stairs. There was a communal shelter nearby but we preferred staying in the house. It was real cosy.

Dad was an ARP warden who was called out on any alert. The fact that we had a car, a Morris Oxford, meant he was doubly important in his role as it could be used as an ambulance and a taxi. Normally we only used it on a Saturday and Sunday because of the petrol shortage but in his job as a warden he got extra supplies to be used, and they were very strict, on official business only.

Harry Tweedy was very proud of his Morris Oxford car which was used as an ambulance and a taxi during the war. He is seen here on the running board alongside his son Arnold. His daughter, Joan, is in the driver's seat.

I can remember during an alert my Mam and I getting him ready with his uniform and tin hat to cycle to my Aunt's in Wenslydale Terrace where the car was garaged. He then drove to Bebside School which was being used as the headquarters for the wardens and ambulance people.

One particular night when a raid was on we were huddled under the stairs when we heard a pounding on the door. It was our local warden telling us to get out of the house as there was an unexploded parachute mine in Ridley Park about a hundred yards away. I dread to think what might have happened if it exploded.

When we got outside we found a bus in the back lane which took us and everyone in the immediate area away from the bomb. Some were taken to stay in the Welfare Hall in Renwick Road but we were able to stop the night with our Aunt Jenny in Lynn Street then the next night with another aunt in Second Avenue.

After the army had dealt with the mine we were allowed back into our homes. That was the night of the bombing of Blyth railway station and I often think that bomb in Ridley Park could well have been dropped by the same German plane.

The next day I was on my way to the Weslyan Church in Waterloo Road when I saw a set of heavy railway bogey wheels lying there. They had been blown several hundred yards by the blast and on seeing the damage to all the houses around it we were very lucky indeed that our bomb did not explode.

Travelling by buses during the war was a trying experience. It was obvious the better buses has been taken over by the forces because all that ran on the local routes were the real wrecks. I can remember on a number of occasions putting up my brolly in the bus because the windows were all broken and the rain was bleaching in.

Another point of contention was that regular travellers from Blyth to Newcastle bought twelve journey tickets which lasted a week. But those that were paying what was known as "full fare" had priority getting on which meant on some occasions having to wait for the next bus.

Jim Derbyshire's Memories:

I was not very old when we moved from Single Row in South Newsham to 15 South View, over the first crossings in Plessey Road, and it was there at the age of seven I had my first taste of war close at hand.

It was in 1941 and our row of houses backed on to the Blyth Golf Course, that was the old twelve hole one, quite a nice view but not so nice when the German raiders came over. I don't know why it was nobody in our street fancied going into the shelters but it seemed everyone preferred their own beds.

I was in bed with my two older stepbrothers, Billy and John Eadington whose Mother, who was widowed, had married my Dad. My two sisters, Joan and Dorothy, were in another bedroom. Offspring of families in those days had to share beds as there weren't any four or five bedroomed council houses available. It was about two o'clock in the morning when a tremendous explosion woke us up. I opened my eyes to find I was looking through the roof at stars and the whole room was filled with dust and rubble.

Three of us started crying with the shock and my Mum and Dad rushed into the room to find out if we were alright. We had a few cuts and bruises as did my sisters whose room was just as damaged.

My Dad then tried to get us all out but the stairs were blocked with the front door which had been blown up the staircase. We managed to manoeuvre the door out of the way and although me and my stepbrothers were just in our shirt tails – we couldn't afford pyjamas in those days, no-one could, – we got out of the house.

We weren't alone in the street as lots of our neighbours were standing outside as well for nearly every house in South View had been damaged and the families bombed out. Dad took us to stay in his parents house in Plessey Road.

The next day we all went back to see the damage. Numbers four, six and eight were nearest the blast, caused by a parachute bomb, which landed on the golf course. They were the worst damaged but none of the houses could be lived in and we were all given alternative accommodation in various empty houses. We went to a terraced house in South Newsham. It was pulled down many years ago. We stayed there for six months and then transferred to 27 Park Drive, also in Newsham.

After the bombing it was then just a question of carrying on. Me and my brothers went back to school as though nothing had happened, Dad went back to work at Wrights Timber Yard. But needless to say shelters became popular after the near miss. As everything was being geared towards the war effort there was no chance of South View being rebuilt until it was over. Blyth Council eventually rebuilt the houses and gave the bombed out families a chance of moving back. We did but it was to a house built immediately opposite where we had lived.

One of my memories is of watching a dogfight over Blyth between a Spitfire and an ME 109 which led to the German being shot down. The pilot parachuted out and, although I did not see it, he was marched through the town watched by hundreds who made their feelings felt through catcalls and boos.

The parachute mine which landed on the Signal Box killing the signalman caused tremendous damage in the surrounding area. Fortunately no-one else was killed but there were a number of casualties – several of them seriously injured. Groups of railwaymen were brought into Blyth to clear the damage from the lines to try and get the station opened again. They can been seen in the picture already working. The Newcastle to Blyth line was a vital link in sustaining supplies to the submarine base and the other army installations in the town.

Bomb Drops

Official reports after the war said other bombings included a mine which had exploded in Blyth Harbour on November 3rd, 1941, two bombs being dropped on Front Street, Bebside and two unexploded parachute mines found at Horton Grange. It was reported they were a new type and of great interest to the bomb disposal experts who were called. In the same raid a bomb seriously damaged a large bomb shelter in the town causing it to collapse. Two shelter marshals, George Evans and Jack Furness, used their bodies as a bridge to help most of the occupants to escape. Four who couldn't get out were rescued uninjured later.

Blyth's Only Victoria Cross

Richard Been Stannard was born in Middleton Street, Blyth, in 1902 the son of Captain George Stannard. He was the eldest of three boys and two girls and attended like his siblings, Crofton Junior School in the town. He was known as a "grand scrapper" at the Royal Naval Merchant School before entering the Merchant Navy at the age of 15. The older staff remember him as an outstanding character who, on one occasion, had a fight with an older boy which lasted forty minutes. Dickie Stannard achieved international fame in 1940 for his exploits as captain of an armed trawler during the Norwegian campaign launched against the Germans invaders for which he was awarded the Victoria Cross. He is the only holder of the award to come from Blyth. Tribute to Dickie Stannard was paid in the columns of the Evening Chronicle by the late Eric Forster during a series on North East VC's. This is what he wrote.

Dickie Stannard, son of a mariner, was destined for the sea. Its influence lay all around him. From his classroom desk in Crofton School, Blyth, he would hear the whoop of ships' sirens. He could walk around the harbour, listen to foreign sailors, watch the little colliers load cargo at the staithes.

He would stare out to the far sea horizons and imagine what lay beyond. At home in Middleton Street, Blyth, there were letters and mementoes from foreign ports, sent home by his father, Captain George Davis Stannard.

The sea was part of the boy. It was inevitable that he, too, would one day become a seaman but meanwhile there were studies to pursue and tasks to perform.

There was nothing to mark him out from his generation unless it was a predilection for getting into scrapes. There were antics which held no malice – but he was always the lad who would dare do that which baulked others.

Inevitably he earned a nickname, "Daredevil Dickie", coined by his friends. Dickie, the eldest of five, would retain that venturesome attitude throughout his life. It would survive hardship. It would survive even the unexplained death of his father who sailed out of New York in command of the Mount Oswald in February, 1912, and was never seen again. The ship vanished in mid-Atlantic.

Richard Stannard.

It had been heartbreaking for him at the age of 12, two years after his father's death, to leave behind his friends in Blyth to go to the Royal Naval Merchant School at Wokingham but he always maintained his contact with Blyth and continued to do so when he joined his first ship at the age of fifteen.

His progress was good. He took his master's certificate at an early age and by the time the Second World War broke out he was second officer on the Orient liner *Orfor*. That then was the boy from Blyth who, in April, 1940, found himself detailed to sail to Norway on an emergency mission. In the interim much had happened to Richard Been Stannard. He had joined the Royal Naval Reserve in 1927. Came the outbreak of war and he was immediately mobilised and placed in command of a … trawler! True, it was an armed trawler with anti-aircraft guns mounted on the deck but it still represented an immense change of command for a man more used to sailing aboard passenger liners.

The difference lay in the fact that this was his own ship, his own command and on his decisions would rest the lives of his crew. He was now Lieutenant Stannard, RNR, bearing on his sleeve the interwoven gold rings of the reservist and, trawler though it be, it was now officially known as His Majesty's Ship 'Arab'. And HMS *Arab*, heaving through storms in the North Sea, was on its way to war.

Dickie Stannard did not know what lay ahead and no-one could tell him but at that moment in April, 1940, the British Army was taking its first reverse. The troops had been landed in Norway in anticipation of Hitler's invasion. Now, beaten back, they were falling on to the coastline and looked to the likes of HMS *Arab* to pluck them back to safety. It was the first Dunkirk.

Lt. Stannard was heading for Namsos. The weather was bad – heaving seas, sleet, freezing winds and sub-zero temperatures – but HMS *Arab* was used to such conditions. The port of Namsos loomed out of the grey mist and Stannard faced, for the first time in his life, the problems of commanding a ship under fire. Ashore there was the flash of field guns and enemy aircraft streamed overhead. Through his field glasses he could see ashore the scurrying uniforms of the men he had come to rescue – soldiers of the retreating army.

Arab nosed its way into harbour in a hail of fire, just as the German bombers arrived to pound the wharf with high explosives. The wharf was loaded with British explosives, including many tons of hand grenades.

Dickie Stannard had already assessed that the wharf was the only possible landing place on the immediate coastline. He did not hesitate. He kept the ship firmly pointed ahead and ran the bows of the *Arab* right into it. The bombing raids had cut off water supplies from ashore but Stannard could see the danger of stacked boxes of grenades exploding and demolishing the entire wharf. He ordered all but two of his crew to the safety of the stern then personally led his volunteers forward to stream the ship's hoses onto the flames.

Two Hour Fight

They kept up the fight for two hours but the task was too great. He ordered the ship to go astern and then navigated it to the other side of the wharf to a point below the pier where *Arab* could take troops aboard.

The air attacks were incessant now and *Arab* had just taken on board its first passengers when the weakened pier began to subside. The logical decision was to pull back, call it a day, think of other means of getting the troops aboard. What he did was to order the ship astern then full steam ahead to ram the bows again under the collapsing structure to shore it up while more troops got aboard.

The attacks from the air intensified but more troops were plucked to safety before the collapsing structure threatened to engulf the ship. He pulled back and saw that enemy planes seemed to be concentrating their attacks on other ships trying to pinion them in one part of the harbour to sink them. Lt. Stannard ordered his gun crew into the attack. *Arab* took a direct hit but sailed on. Dive bombers were now taking up the attack and one stitched a line of bullets across the ship one of them ripping through his right hand as he gripped a rail. He said nothing but took out a handkerchief and knotted it around the wound with his teeth.

He headed the *Arab* towards the shelter of a cliff face which offered some defence against the diving bombers. There he put his crew ashore to establish an armed base to which retreating solders could head for shelter and pick up. It was strategically a brilliant move. His own guns could direct fire at the attacking plains which could not get close enough to mount their own attacks.

The abortive raid on Namos in Norway led to many deaths among the British attackers. The raid was later called the first Dunkirk because of the need to evacuate the survivors.

Dickie Stannard manned the base for two days but still more troops were falling back and looking to him for both defence and rescue. He did not fail them at one point having the ships guns taken ashore and mounted along the cliff to offer cover for the troops.

In total the *Arab*, its crew and passengers, suffered 31 attacks in which only one man was injured. Continuously he scanned the shore in a search for British uniforms. He saw one company of Sherwood Foresters wiped out. Another group, dragging their wounded, made it to his armed camp. They proved to be the last.

Stannard was now suffering from frostbite in his feet but made light of it as he nosed *Arab* away

Blyth News

Ashington Post

's and Thursdays

THURSDAY, SEPTEMBER 5, 1940.

0

ONE

Establis

Blyth V.C. Hero at The Palace

While an air raid was in progress, the King, on Tuesday morning decorated Lieut - Commander Richard Stannard, R.N.R., of Blyth, with the V.C. at an investiture at Buckingham Palace. Lieut.-Commander Stannard (centre) is seen (right) leaving the Palace after the investiture and (below) congratulating 2nd Lieut. R. W. Annand of South Shields, who had also received the V.C.

from the sheltering cliffs. Immediately he was under attack. A neighbouring ship took a direct hit and burst into flames. It threatened to explode at any second but Dick Stannard went alongside, called for volunteers, then leapt aboard to rescue what crew he could. He then cut the *Arab* free. Only one hundred yards separated him from the burning ship when it exploded and sank.

He now set a course for home but the ordeal was not yet over. He was just drawing free of the fjord when a German bomber veered towards his ship, assessed it as damaged and harmless and signalled him to alter course to the east or be sunk. He ignored the order and chugged on at a steady four knots.

The bomber swooped in low on a bombing run and when it was 800 yards away he ordered his crew to open fire. The first burst sent the plane spinning down into the sea. The battered *Arab* then sailed into home port to tremendous public acclaim and four months later the Blyth born lad all knew as Daredevil Dickie went to Buckingham Palace to receive his VC from King George VI. He also received the Royal Norwegian War Cross from King Haakin in the same year.

Two years later, by now in command of an aging destroyer called Vimy and with memories of Dunkirk and Atlantic convoy duties behind him Dickie was again pushed into the thick of major battle. The occasion was a pitched battle between packs of U-boats and a major convoy. It lasted for 72 hours. At least three U-boats were destroyed and among the victors was Dick Stannard. Amazingly, it was back to Buckingham Palace again, this time to have a DSO ribbon added to the dark purple of his VC. The war ended and Dickie went back to the job he loved with the Orient line. No bombs, no shelling, no lurking submarines, no raiding aircraft. He ranged the world but never lost touch with his native Blyth. One old friend said: "He always called to see us – still the same laughing Dickie we knew at school."

When his life at sea on liners came to an end Dick Stannard was appointed Marine Superintendent for the Orient Line based in Sidney, Australia, where he settled until his death in 1976 at the age of 74. Since then his valour has been recognised in Blyth by the naming of the Stannard Room at the Civic Centre and the new Stannard Building in Bridge Street. He is also recognised by the Royal Naval Reserve with the Stannard Room in their headquarters in Lowestoft which is dedicated to "the glorious memory of Lt. Commander Richard Stannard VC".

Richard Baker, the well known BBC broadcaster, tells interesting tales about the time he served as a midshipman aboard the destroyer Vimy when Dickie Stannard was captain. Apparently his skipper took great pride in always being smartly turned out and in order to make sure his "whites" were immaculate got them clean by towing them behind the ship. And when he heard that Richard Baker played the piano had one brought on board so the future popular broadcaster could entertain the crew.

The PLR School Head

Lord Glenamara, better known in Blyth as Ted Short, is now 97 and living in a residential home in Hexham. His marriage to Jenny, which produced two children, Michael and June, ended after 68 years with her death two years ago. Ted Short had four careers – teaching, the army, politics and heading an international communications company. This is the story of his teaching career in Blyth.

The newly appointed headmaster of Princess Louise Road Secondary Modern School in Blyth had just finished a five year stint as a captain in the Durham Light Infantry during the Second World War when he arrived at his new civvies posting. He found the corridor walls covered in rude graffiti and every book in the school which had pictures also contained obscene drawings.

Looking back he says: "The school was in complete chaos and I immediately regretted what I had taken on. It was a nightmare. The school had not been painted nor had any money been spent on it for many years. It was in a shocking state, a complete contrast to the school I taught in at Forest Hall before the war."

It was September the First, 1947, and Ted Short, later to be enobled as Lord Glenamara, found the first day at his new job coincided with the introduction of the new Education Act which raised the leaving age to fifteen.

"This meant I had a large group of 14-year-olds staying on instead of leaving with the new influx of youngsters from the junior schools flooding in," he said. "As we only had eight classrooms and accommodation for half classes in the woodwork and metalwork sections we had far too many pupils, indeed as many as fifty to a class. Every seat in the school was taken.

The prefects of Princess Louise Road Secondary Modern School pictured with their headmaster, Ted Short, later to become Lord Glenamara in the school yard in 1950. Back row: Ron Stanbury, Alan Oram, Cyril Atkinson. Front row: Peter Tilmouth, Les Allen, Alex Robbie, Ted Short, Jim Harland, George Fulcher and Terry Rutherford.

"The education authorities in their wisdom did provide me with extra staff for the additional numbers but they all turned out to be trainees from a one-year emergency training course which had been rushed through by the Government. They had no experience of standing in front of a class or indeed knowing what they had to teach." Worse was to follow for the new head as he found no programmes of work had been arranged for the pupils and that discipline was so bad every teacher kept a cane up his or her sleeve and administered corporal punishment when needed.

Princess Louise Road Secondary Modern School in 1950.

The classroom shortage he tackled by taking over a short corridor in the school and installing curtains for privacy, which gave him an additional half classroom, but his plan for a reformation of the corporal punishment system in the school backfired somewhat. He withdrew the canes from all the teachers informing them he was the only one to carry out punishment and that any miscreant was to be sent to him.

The cane he found in the previous head's cupboard was soon in action but he was overwhelmed by the numbers sent from the classrooms, sometimes a dozen at a time.

"I was at my wits end and decided to reissue the canes to the staff," he said. "I restored the power to the teacher on the strict understanding every punishment and the reason for it had to be recorded and sent to me."

Despite the use of the cane there were still instances of vandalism. He introduced magic lantern show programmes in the main hall with the pupils all seated and when it was over the cable to the projector was found to have been cut. All the pupils were marched back into the hall and told to sit exactly where they had been. In this way he found the culprit who then paid for his folly with a visit to the headmaster's office for a caning.

Ted Short introduced regular P.E. classes shortly after arriving at Princess Louise Road School. Here pupils can be found exercising in the school playground in 1950.

It took the new headmaster and his staff over six months to come up with a curriculum for the school which laid down hard and fast the education programme the pupils would get.

Mr. Short's office by this time was becoming rather cluttered as it was being used to store the vandalised books, which could not possibly be used, and it took him some time to persuade the education authority to provide replacements.

One instance which still rankles in his mind is a school inspection barely one year after he took over at the school. He said: "Six inspectors turned up and spent some time at the school. It was grossly unfair considering what had to be done. Their report was good in parts but it should never have taken place when it did."

The senior form at Princess Louise Road Secondary Modern School pictured with their teachers Barty Peel and Alan Smith (seated front row centre) in the school yard in 1950.

Mr. Short had a number of run-ins with the local education officer and sometimes went over his head to County Hall. But he was annoyed when a board of governors was appointed to cover all four senior schools in the town. Head teachers had to go through them if they wanted anything. He was further annoyed when they turned down his appeal for mobile classrooms to help ease the overcrowding and they also, initially, refused to install a telephone in the school.

"It was ludicrous," he said. "There were three schools on our site – ours, the girls and the juniors - and there was not a phone between us. If any of us wanted to make a call on school business we had to go to the nearest public phone box. We had a suspicion the governors felt it would be abused by the staff."

Another of the innovations he managed to get past the governors eighteen months after he joined was the installation of a kitchen by taking over a small area in the woodwork and metalwork section.

"Our pupils who qualified for school dinners had to use St. Wilfrid's school hall which was across the road from us," he said. "As we had some 450 pupils it seemed only right we should have our own catering."

In his effort to improve things at the school he introduced a school crest and motto – *Ad Meliore* – To Better Things – and a house system – Lion, Stag, Dragon and Eagle – which brought about friendly, competitive rivalry among the pupils. He also appointed a head boy and prefects and brought in a voluntary school blazer and a flagpole erected in the playground to fly flags on saint's days and royal birthdays. The introduction of a Parents Teachers Association also proved to be highly successful and extremely helpful. Getting the name of the school altered was one of his failures. He felt it was wrong to be called Princess Louise Road Secondary Modern School and that the "road" should be dropped and indeed wrote to Kensington Palace requesting a portrait of Princess Louise. It was duly received and displayed in the school but it had no effect. Even to this day it is still PLR.

Mr. Short rated Bart Peel and Johnny Jures as two of his best teachers and said he had a high regard for most of the pupils. But he also had great annoyance that some of them were being short-changed in their education because of the 11-plus examination which determined which school, secondary modern or secondary grammar, they went to.

"It was a system which did not rely on ability but on the number of places the secondary schools, later grammar schools, had. Eighty per cent did not get a place and because of that were labelled failures which they were most definitely not. But it is a label which I know still rancours with many of them today."

It was in his second career as a politician that Ted Short was able to help get rid of the 11-plus. He was a member of the Wilson government which agreed to scrap it without it going through Parliament.

"Tony Crosland, the Secretary of State for Education, sent out letters to every local authority telling them the examination was unfair and they should phase it out and they did," he recalls.

The teaching staff at Princess Louise Road Secondary Modern School in 1950. Back row: Ken Jones, Octave Castiaux, Fred Wilson and Alan Bennett. Front row: Alan Smith, Johnny Jures, Jack Tweddle, Ted Short, Barty Peel, Robert Todd and Jack Graham.

Ted Short, who was also a local councillor in Newcastle while in teaching, left Princess Louise school after four years on being elected to Parliament for Newcastle Central where his drive and ability got him many senior posts. Under Harold Wilson he served as Secretary of State for Education, Postmaster General, leader of the House of Commons, Chief Whip, Deputy Leader and Lord President of the Council. He was not offered a place in the Callaghan government when Harold Wilson retired and left the Commons on January 28th, 1977, to take a seat in the House of Lords as Lord Glenamara of Glenridding.

At the same time he was appointed chairman of the nationalised Cable and Wireless Ltd, a position he held for three years until 1980 when ill health led to him stepping down.

He became active again on Tyneside being made chancellor of the University of Newcastle until 2005 four years after he was made a Freeman of Newcastle.

He says: "In the whole of my life the two most difficult jobs I had were the four years at Princess Louise school and running the Chief Whips Office in Parliament when we only had a majority of three."

The Death of Cinema in Blyth

Peter Douglas, the long serving projectionist at the Wallaw Cinema walked on to the stage at 10.45 on the night of Thursday the 29th of April, 2004. Watched by twenty people standing in the circle he was about to bring to an end cinema in the town which had lasted over 100 years and at one time boasted five cinemas at its peak.

Peter Douglas.

Peter had had the option of closing the curtains for the final time from the projection booth or by pressing the button on the side of the stage but it was deemed by the assembly that it was only fitting the ceremony was done from the stage. The final spool of Mel Gibson's *The Passion of Christ* had run out half an hour earlier and there had been no problems at all with any of the equipment.

In the circle glasses were raised in tribute after Peter's short address and he disappeared into the wings to press the button. The whir of the motor started and the golden curtains slowly began to close for the last time. Then, as if instructed by some other force, they stopped halfway through the task never to restart.

One of the onlookers said: "It's the Wallaw ghost. It doesn't want it to close."

The cinema was built on the site of a Victorian circus and it was rumoured that a circus hand had been killed during one of the performances early in the century when a weight dropped on his head and that his ghost walked the building. Now having acted as manager for over a year and having been in the building at the most peculiar hours with the place in complete darkness I can honestly say I never saw or heard the ghost.

Ghost or not we later found that the wire controlling the curtains had come off its track and so it was that the Wallaw closed finally with the curtains half shut.

The frontage of the Wallaw Cinema in Union Street shortly after its conversion to triple screens.

After the theatre was left in darkness many people expressed to me their sorrow that it was closed. My reply was: "When did you last buy a ticket?" That, unfortunately, was the trouble. We could stand in the foyer and watch people park their cars in front of the cinema, walk across Union Street and hire videos from a shop on the corner.

The Wallaw had a chequered career since being built in 1937. It had a stable ownership until Walter Lawson (Wal-law), who had built it, sold it to the ABC chain in 1955. In 1966, with the permanent closure of the Theatre Royal, Blyth Operatic Society moved its annual show there despite having only a 12 foot deep stage to work on.

The building changed hands yet again in 1970 being taken over by Sol Sheckman owner of the giant Essoldo chain. Two years later he sold it on to Classic Cinemas who kept it for only five years when a Berwick businessman took charge. He closed it for a while before re-opening in 1982. When again threatened with closure Eddie Ferguson, the owner of Ferguson's Transport and President of Blyth Amateur Operatic Society, bought the cinema in 1984 to ensure the Society could continue their live performances there.

He then leased the cinema to the partnership of Bob Milner and Peter Lish and the lease included a provision that it be made available to the Society. At the time it was one cinema with over 1,400 seats but the new lessees converted it into three cinemas by bringing a wall down from the front of the circle to form the 80 seat Mini and 150 seat Minor with the Major now down to 850 seats.

Bob incidentally was the St. Mary's church organist and installed a modern organ for a time at the cinema which he played as part of the evening's entertainment.

In addition, while using the former sweet shop attached to the building as a publicity and ticket office, I introduced live professional shows to the theatre. Ken Dodd was one of the stars who filled the place as did Ronnie Hilton and Ruby Murray. Ruby, who is no longer with us, had a drink problem and agents would not book her because of her failure to fulfill engagements.

Ruby Murray.

I booked her direct and I can say she was perfectly behaved. She turned up on time, was sober and gave a great performance. It was only after she finished her act in the first half that I found her consuming the hard stuff in the dressing room. All I can say is that I found her a real lady.

Other stars who appeared were Danny La Rue, John Inman, the Roly Polys, Edmund Hockridge and Hinge and Bracket. My memory of the late Danny was when he invited me to try on one of his dresses in his dressing room – an invitation I politely declined.

Danny La Rue.

Two current millionaire TV stars who made their stage debut at the Wallaw were a couple of young men called P.J. and Duncan, stars of Byker Grove, later to adopt their real names Ant and Dec. At the time they had released a record which was being promoted and came as part of a rock and roll package put together by a Newcastle impresario. Their stage debut lasted just over six minutes – long enough for them to sing both sides of the record!

Another show which filled the place was a VE Day Celebration. As a gimmick I printed the programmes on my office copier in the form of a wartime ration book. There were over 850 in the theatre and we printed 400 programmes – more than enough, we thought. Such was the demand for them as souvenirs we had to print another 200 to distribute at the interval.

Another Change

When Bob Milner moved to Blackpool in 2002 a Scottish couple, Brian and Jeanette Lough, who ran a cinema in a former church in Kelso took over the lease. They soon found, apart from school holidays, that the apathy among adults in the town meant it was losing money. Mind you the Wallaw was not the most solubrious of places to visit. Money for refurbishment which needed to be invested in the three cinemas and foyer was not available. In addition vandalism became prevalent because of having to operate with the minimum of staff. The days of staff with torches showing you to your seat and remaining in the cinema had long gone

The interior of the Major cinema in the Wallaw which is Grade Two listed because of its art deco appearance.

When the building was converted into three screens it could only be done if there were individual projection rooms. In multi-screen cinemas nowadays one projection room handles all the screens. At the Wallaw

Peter Douglas became the fittest projectionist in the country.

The times of starting had to be staggered to allow Peter to service all three projectors. The Mini was downstairs with the projection room alongside. The Minor projection room was at the bottom of the rear stairs which could only be accessed by a run up the stairs, across the upstairs foyer and down the rear stairs. The Major, on the top floor, was got to by an iron circular staircase, very tricky to navigate when carrying large boxes containing the film reels.

This meant the three rooms could not be manned at the same time. On one occasion two youths from the Wellesley Campus, used by Sunderland Council to re-educate truculent youngsters, were seen acting suspiciously before hurriedly leaving the building. On going into the Minor projection room I discovered they had cut the film as it was running through the machine. Fortunately they cut it after it had been through the gate and the film continued to be shown on screen as a huge pile of film built up on the floor.

There had already been prior trouble with youngsters from Wellesley who were breaking into the frames outside the cinema and stealing the posters. As a result all Wellesley youngsters were banned from the building. There was also the defacing of the seats, particularly in the Minor which had a cloth covering and was easily written on. The Mini, with velum covering, was where the slashings took place but fortunately there were plenty of spare seats hidden in many of the numerous rooms in the building following the conversion.

The last live show was the March, 2004, production of South Pacific by the Blyth Operatic Society. The closure also affected the Beaconsfield Operatic Society which was by then an October regular and they moved with the Blyth Society to the Phoenix Theatre in Beaconsfield Street with its small stage and 300 seat auditorium.

The First Theatre

The first recorded theatre in Blyth was in 1870 in Bridge Street and was the Theatre Royal later to become the Alexandra Billiard Hall in 1907. The etched glass doors marking the stalls and circle were still evident in the 1970's before it was eventually demolished to make way for the Mall Shopping Centre.

The Theatre Royal in Trotter Street opened initially as the New Theatre in 1900 and later showed films in an effort to make it viable financially. It was demolished in the 1980s.

The Central Hall in the Market Place came into being in 1857 but was burnt down in 1923 and two years later re-opened as the Central Cinema with 1,400 seats. It operated as a cinema until July, 1961, when it turned to Bingo and was demolished in 1974 after standing derelict for some years.

The Essoldo in Beaconsfield Street was always regarded as the best cinema in the town and was built on the site of the Empire, which had opened in 1911 with over 1,000 seats, and closed in 1937 when it was demolished to make way for the Essoldo. The new cinema had 1,700 seats and featured in the town until November 1973 when it closed. Five years later it re-opened as a skate board centre. It closed again some months later and was demolished in 1980 when Blyth Central Methodist Church, which had sold its Bridge Street church to the developers of the Mall, was built on the site.

In 1910 the first purpose built cinema in Blyth, the Empire was opened in Beaconsfield Street on the site on which the new Methodist Church now stands. Sol Sheckman of Essoldo fame took it over in 1933 but closed it in 1937 to allow the new Essoldo, Blyth, to be built. It was opened in July, 1938. The building to the right of the picture used to be long-established Hedley Young's but is now the home of a Poundstretcher shop.

The Hippodrome in Post Office Square was built in 1907 as a theatre and was originally a wooden building. It later became a skating rink until it was converted into a cinema with 1,200 seats in 1920 and operated until its closure in 1940. I can recall going to the Hippodrome in 1939 as a four-year-old and while I cannot remember what I saw my elder sibling tells me you could get in with an empty jam jar which were quite valuable at the time. At the time of its closure the foundations were laid for another cinema but because of the war construction on the old Hippodrome site did not begin until 1954. The new Roxy Cinema opened a year later alongside the Roxy Ballroom and Cafe, which was already well established.

The Theatre Royal in Trotter Street, was also equipped to show films and this had been attempted by the Essoldo company, which owned it, when live repertory failed to draw but without success. It had been closed three years until the Blyth Operatic Society reopened it with a production of the *White Horse Inn* and sold every seat for the whole week.

The fifth purpose built cinema in the town with 450 seats, was the Plaza on Newcastle Road, Newsham which opened in 1937. Known locally as the flea pit I recall on my visits there to see the Flash Gordon serials on a Saturday afternoon you made quite certain you went early to make sure you were seated at the back of the steeply raked auditorium. The reason for this was because of the reluctance of young patrons to use the official toilets in case they lost their seats to latecomers. This resulted in a constant stream of urine running down to the front of the cinema despite numerous pleas from the management.

When cinema going went out of fashion the Plaza stood empty for a while until it was converted into a Methodist Chapel. When that closed in 2005 it was taken over as the New Hope Church.

Films still can be seen on occasions in Blyth Valley through a touring company called Doorstep Pictures, part of the Tyneside Cinema, which makes one-day visits to put on the latest films in community centres in Seaton Sluice, New Hartley and the Isabella in Ogle Drive, Blyth.

The Blyth Operatic Society's cast of 'The Desert Song' on stage at the Theatre Royal in March 1963, two years before the theatre closed forever.

The leading players in the 'White Horse Inn' which re-opened the Theatre Royal in 1962 after being closed for three years. From left to right: Ted Hogg, Pearl Powell, Jimmy Russell, Nancy Haxon, Jim Harland, Mildred Eadington and Eric Lambert.

Part of the cast of the 'Sound of Music' on stage after the final performance of the show in 1973 which attracted 8,221 customers during the week's run – a record for the Wallaw cinema.

The Central Hall, later to be rebuilt as the Central Cinema, in Blyth Market Place with the Zion Methodist Church spire on the left. The drinking fountain (centre right) is believed to be in the grounds of a private house in the Morpeth area.

The Unsung Blyth Spartans Man

Many words have been written about the heroic FA Cup exploits of Blyth Spartans. The chairman, the manager and the players have all received their plaudits on television, radio and in newspapers. But one man who contributed as much and possibly, on occasions, even more to the success of the Spartans has been the unsung hero, George Watson, the secretary of the football side from 1967 until 1990. Who knows, but had George been a little taller he could well have played in goal for his favourite team. This is the story of the ups and downs of the Croft Park club during his time there.

George Watson was born in 157 Twentieth Avenue, Blyth, on September 26th, 1937, to Jack and Jenny Watson and was educated at Princess Louise Road Infants, Crofton Junior and Blyth Secondary Grammar.

It was in Crofton school he came to the attention of one of the masters, Ernie Leask, a fanatic about schools football, who picked him for the Under 10's school team as a fullback, then the Under 11's as a right winger but in the Grammar school Under 15's he ended up as a goalkeeper.

And it was as a shot stopper he was recommended at the senior school for trials with the Town's Under 13's side. It was run, as it so happens, by his former mentor, Ernie Leask, and he quickly put George back on the right wing, but under a new manager of the Under 15's he was back in goal for the Blyth side.

"I was a good goalkeeper but I was never going to make anything of it because of my height" he says. He also turned out for Seaton Delaval Juniors and won many East Northumberland League trophies but opted out of moving into senior football and gave up playing

George Watson, aged 10.

From the age of sixteen George had been an avid supporter of the Spartans watching the likes of Harry Mills, who later went professional with Huddersfield, Billy Fenwick and Gavin Gair as well as the Turney brothers, Jim and Frankie.

Crofton Junior School football team, 1947-48. Back row: Mr Howes, Mr Leask. Middle row: John Levy, Alan Lawton, Tony Johnson, Tom Miles, Brian Illingworth, Joe Ball, George Watson. Front row: Roland Bell, Gordon Watson, John Windle, Donald Eadington and Allan Short.

George served for a time on the committee of the Supporters Club but he was twenty eight before he joined the board of the Spartans and in 1967 took over as the football secretary. At the time, with the folding of the semi-professional North Eastern League in 1962, Blyth was in the Northern League, although it had played for a time in the Midland League where long trips involved visits to places like Peterborough.

The Northern League was amateur but it was well known that "expenses" the players were allowed to claim could be plentiful and indeed, cash was often placed in a player's boot.

George tells of the time when one "amateur" in Durham turned down the chance of joining Chelsea because of the "expenses" he was on with a well-known club which played in the Amateur Cup. A Blyth-born player, also with the Durham club, declined to join the Spartans for the same reason.

George soon found being secretary had its problems. A chairman was elected from the committee annually and some were extremely difficult to contact on occasions. He mentions one whom he needed to get an urgent decision from.

Rang Wife

"It was in the evening and when I rang his home his wife told me although she knew where he was he could not be contacted," he said. "I told her it was of extreme importance and I had to speak to him. Eventually after much persuasion she gave me a telephone number and said I had to destroy it after use.

"I rang the number and spoke to a very guarded man. The chairman eventually came to the phone and the first thing he said on being told who it was: 'Where did you get this number from?' He was at a meeting of the Freemasons in Beaconsfield Street!"

Continuity came for George when the board scrapped the one-year terms and Jim Turney took over as the head in the early 70's, a position he held for the next eighteen years.

The new secretary though had to wait almost four years before he tasted big success in the FA Cup. It was in the 1971-72 season that the Spartans disposed of Crewe in the first round, Stockport in the second and met Reading in the third. Immediately after defeat by Blyth the managers of Crewe and Stockport, Dennis Violet and Billy Wood, had been sacked. On the eve of Reading's visit to Blyth Charlie Hurley, the former Sunderland favourite, was appointed manager of the southern club.

When he arrived at Croft Park he saw the figure of a dummy hanging by a rope from the stand bearing the placard "Sorry Charlie, you're next!" But Charlie had the last

The Blyth Spartans squad involved in the historic 1977/78 cup run.

laugh for following a draw Reading trounced the Spartans 6-l in the replay on their ground.

It was five years later Blyth Spartans had their historic run which took them into the hat for the sixth round draw and a possible tie with the mighty Arsenal.

The 1977-78 season saw the Spartans put paid to the cup hopes of Shildon, Crook, Consett, Bishop Auckland, Burscough, Chesterfield, Enfield and Stoke City. Even now George still bristles at the treatment the Spartans received from the league club.

"There are some professional sides which treat you like kings when you visit but there are others who look down on you as though you had no right to be there. Stoke was one such. On two occasions they allowed us to travel when the prospect of the game being staged was doubtful. On the first occasion they did not call the referee to inspect an waterlogged pitch and fifteen coaches carrying our fans were turned back by the police on the motorway.

"On the second occasion four days later we were already in our hotel in Manchester when I got a call from their secretary that the game was off. It was only later I was told by Ronnie Clark of the Supporters Club, that they had heard of the postpostment on the radio before us. Stoke had told the media before informing us."

John Ryman M.P.

The third attempt to play the game was successful on February 6th, 1978, and it was a match which saw John Ryman the Blyth M.P. put his foot right in it. As the Spartans cup-winning exploits were getting headlines Ryman, a London barrister, decided he would attend the match. Stoke, lying 14th in the English Second Division, lost 3-2 and the M.P. was one of the Blyth contingent who went in to the board room after the match.

George says: "The room was crowded but it was also deadly silent. Ryman's first clanger came when everyone heard him commiserating with the Stoke chairman by saying: 'I do not understand your attitude you gave us a very hard game'."

The remark was met in stunned silence but not his second clanger. Newcastle United were playing Wrexham in the cup and if the Magpies won then Blyth would be playing them in the next round. The result came through – Wrexham had won.

George recounts: "The MP's response to our disappointment was 'Oh well, it's just up the Tyne Valley'. There were hoots of laughter all round and someone told him that it was Wrexham in Wales not Hexham on Tyne. By this time there were loud chants outside calling for the Stoke board and the manager to resign.

"Actually we were rather apprehensive about what might happen to us as our coach was parked immediately outside the main entrance but I have to compliment the Stoke fans. Not only did they applaud us on to the coach but some of them came aboard to shake our hands. They treated us like royalty."

The fifth round saw the infamous corner flag incident at Wrexham when the referee gave a

Blyth Spartans v Wrexham match programme at St. James' Park.

corner which was later shown should not have been awarded. He then allowed the kick to be taken three times as the corner flag kept falling down. It allowed the Welsh side to equalise and force a replay at St. James' Park.

On February 27th, 1978, a crowd of 42,000 poured in to the ground to watch the Spartans try and win through to a sixth round tie with Arsenal. A further 10,000 were locked out including many who had tickets. The Spartans lost 2-1 and Wrexham went to Highbury.

George explained: "It was the police who ordered the gates closed as there were hordes running from one turnstile to another trying to get in. At the end of the game Hazel, the wife of our coach Jacky Marks told me her husband was crying and I replied he was not the only one.

"Roy Caller, of the Callers Pegasus travel firm, told us afterwards he would contact the Arsenal and see if we could play them in a pre-season friendly and he would pay all the

*George Watson,
aged 72.*

expenses. Unfortunately it did not happen as Arsenal were not prepared to play their first team, just their reserves."

The fabulous cup run had hit the headlines all over the world. Even the Tokyo Times, George said, had a piece on their front page and for weeks afterwards cuttings from foreign papers arrived at Croft Park.

Biggest Transfer

The cup run certainly helped the club financially as it cleared £36,000 after expenses, and it helped three Spartans player move in to football full time. Steve Carney and Alan Shoulder were both signed by Newcastle and Keith Houghton for Carlisle. But George reveals they only received one transfer fee – that was £10,000 for Shoulder.

"As Steve and Keith were not contracted we got no fees but Newcastle gave us a £500 'gift' for Steve and said if he proved himself there would be further money. Steve played 104 times for the first team, I think he proved himself, but we didn't get any more cash."

But the biggest transfer Blyth were involved in was after the three FA Cup matches against Hull City in the 1980-81 season. The first two ended in a 1-1 then a 2-2 draw with the decider being played at Elland Road in Leeds.

George said: "Hull won 2-1 and immediately after the game an official of the club came up to me and quizzed me about Les Mutrie. He asked what he worked at and I said he was helping out in a pub. He then said Hull were interested in signing him. I told him I had better call the chairman, Jim Turney.

"The next day Les and Jim travelled down to Hull and a deal was done for £30,000. Tommy Beal our treasurer was delighted when it was arranged we would get £1,000 a month for thirty months. It meant not only that we could avoid tax on such a payment but also he was getting a guaranteed monthly income.

"Unfortunately after about six payments Hull went into receivership and the liquidator said we would be getting no more money. This came as quite a shock but I contacted the Football Association and the Registration Secretary, after hearing my tale, asked me to give him ten minutes. When he rang me back he said we'd be getting the money.

"He then explained that he told the administrator that football rules dictated that a club owing money to another could be suspended immediately and that they had better pay up or Hull would not be allowed to fulfil fixtures. I'm pleased to say we got the next 24 payments and Tommy, and indeed all of us, were happy."

During his time as secretary, which ended in 1990, George Watson served with several managers – Tony Knox, Jacky Marks, Alan Jones, Billy Bell, Brian Slane, Alan O'Neil, Peter Feenan, Michael Dagless and Bobby Elwell.

The camaraderie of the management and the players from the Cup era was shown following the death from cancer of the Spartans defensive stalwart Ronnie Scott at the age of 68. Fifteen ex-players turned out for the funeral at Cowpen Crematorium and eleven former players were on the pitch at Croft Park for a one minutes applause tribute at the home game which followed the service.

George has nothing but the great admiration for Ronnie. "He was a real gentleman. He did not own a car and after some midweek games if he was on the midnight shift at the pit we would arrive back in Blyth on the bus at about eleven and I would then drive him to his home in Broomhill where he changed into his pit gear and then I ran him to the Whittle Colliery. How many footballers would do that now?"

Four months before retiring as secretary of the club George was appointed a lifetime member of the Northumberland Football Association for his work for the sport. And now he spends his time at his home, administrative duties over, in Coronation Street which, coincidentally, backs on to Croft Park.

"It was not a deliberate choice because of it's proximity to the ground but because Margaret and I fancied the house," he said. "It was quite amusing when we were shown around the house by the elderly lady. Taking us in to the back bedroom she whispered conspiratorially: 'And you know you can watch all the matches out of the window free of charge'."

Blyth Spartans may not have won the FA Cup in 1978 but they had several trophies on show in the clubhouse at the end of the season. The late Ronnie Scott (left) is holding the Northern League Cup, skipper John Waterson is cutting the cake presented by their FA cup victors, Wrexham, while Tommy Dixon is holding the Northumberland Senior Cup and Debenham Cup. This cup was played for by the two clubs who played in the first round of the FA Cup and made the furthest progress in the competition. Blyth won the two-legged tie against Wrexham 3-1. Debenham's asked for the solid silver trophy back five years later to give to a golfing competition.

Jacky Marks v Jim Turney

In the previous article George Watson makes reference to Jacky Marks, the Blyth Spartans coach. Jacky, who lives in Wideopen is 78, but still retains a strong love of football and manages to regularly attend soccer matches, league and non-league. Here Jacky tells of the Stoke City FA Cup incident and also his love hate relationship with Jim Turney, the long serving player, manager and chairman of Blyth Spartans.

FA Cup fame for Jacky came quite a long time after he had managed the Spartans and lost his job. He took the helm at Croft Park in 1967 at the princely sum of ten shillings a week but originally had been rejected for the post.

"There were two of us in for it and Tony Knox got it," says Jack. "But after about six or seven weeks he packed it in. He told me he could not put up with the chairman, Jimmy Turney, who had previously held the combined chairman and manager's posts.

"Tony said Jim was interfering in team selection, and hadn't really given him a chance to impose his managerial style on the team. Anyhow I got a call from the chairman asking if I would take over. I said I would, provided I had control over team selection, tactics and the signing of players. He agreed but I soon found out that the ten shillings a week I was getting meant I was subsidising the club as it by no means covered my expenses.

Jacky Marks.

"Eventually I asked the chairman for a rise but he refused and I decided to leave. I told the players in the dressing room after a match at Whitley Bay I was quitting and the reason why. They were all being paid more than me and immediately they said they would chip in and pay me a rise if I stayed. I told them it would not be right and I left despite a later approach by the chairman to stay.

"Almost four years passed when Jim turned up at my work at Winthrop Laboratories where I was site engineer. He said he was planning to appoint Brian Slane as manager but would only do so if I returned as coach. He said he would pay me £5 a week so I agreed."

Jim Turney.

The combination of Jacky, Brian Slane and Billy Fenwick, a former player and long servant of the club, was the catalyst for the Spartans success in the FA Cup where Blyth and Wrexham, who had to replay a fifth round tie, were pulled out of the hat to meet Arsenal in the sixth round draw.

As George Watson said in his article the attitude of Stoke City, who were drawn at home to Blyth in the fourth round, to playing the "minnows" in the cup competition left a lot to be desired.

Jacky takes up the story: "We were drawn away to Stoke and the team bus travelled down on the Friday where we were booked into an hotel near the city. There had been some rain during the week and after training with the lads on the Saturday morning George and I decided to visit the ground.

"On arrival we found it in a terrible state with the ground staff shovelling gallons of water off the pitch. Apparently a stream running alongside the ground had overflowed flooding the pitch. It was obvious to me there was not a chance of the game being played. Their secretary was there and the groundsman and I asked if the referee had been called in to carry out an early inspection.

"They both said, in rather hoity, toity ways, that the referee was due to inspect at one o'clock. I pointed out that fifteen coaches with our fans were already on the way to the Potteries. The reaction of the groundsman and the secretary was "so what". I must admit I saw red and blew up. I have to also admit both the Stoke officials seemed rather frightened at my annoyance but despite rumours to the contrary no-one was assaulted."

The replay was scheduled for the Wednesday and it was here Jim Turney, who was quite a successful business man, showed his more generous side by paying all the expenses of the squad to stay over in the Stoke hotel for the night instead of travelling straight back to the North East.

Jacky said: "The game was postponed again on the Monday but it gave us the greatest of pleasure to beat them when we eventually played, particularly after the way they treated us as if we were village idiots."

Staff at the Stoke ground were still busy sweeping water off the pitch when Blyth officials arrived for an inspection on the morning of the first scheduled game – it led to quite an argument between Jacky Marks, the Spartans coach, and Stoke officials.

Jacky Marks (left) and Brian Slane (extreme right) take their applause during a lap of honour at St. James' Park after their triumphal FA Cup run.

Terry Johnson, Jacky Marks, Dave Clarke and Brian Slane toast the victory at Stoke.

Terry Johnson scoring the winner at Stoke.

Blyth's Only World Champion

Gerry Evans was born in 75 Delaval Terrace on February 21st, 1931. He spent all his working life in the town after being educated at Wright Street Infants, Morpeth Road Junior and Princess Louis Road Senior Schools. He was a keen member of the 4th Blyth Scouts troup based at St Mary's Church and after working as a clerical officer with the National Coal Board became credit controller for Fergusons Transport until his retirement. He was part time leader of Blyth YMCA for 28 years.

Gerry's sporting love was running and his hero was Albert Grant who ran as a professional sprinter under the name W. Spence of Blyth. Albert won the Powderhall Sprint, the blue riband of pro running, in 1947, and three years later took the world professional championship in Australia. As Gerry Evans now explains he is the only world champion to come out of Blyth.

Gerry Evans today.

It was in the scouts that I discovered I could run a bit and I eventually became Blyth Schools 70 yards sprint champion at the schools meeting at Croft Park, home of Blyth Spartans. I also got medals at scout sports and eventually, on leaving school, became a professional sprinter competing in the many galas and flower shows which seemed to be held in all the mining villages. These short sprints paid prizes of up to £50 but a lot more could be made by using the bookies who turned out.

There was a running school at Jacko Smith's running track which was on land near where the Blyth Comrades Club now stands and it was run by Jack McSloy, George Ferry and John Stephens.

It was around this time I made the acquaintance of Albert Grant who had started work as a painter but joined the Royal Navy as a submariner at the outbreak of was. It was then he showed his first burst of speed when he beat the Royal Navy sprint champion wearing plimsolls. On his discharge from the navy he took up a professional sprint career and accepted an invitation from the top trainer Tommy Potter of Carlisle to be "prepped" for the 1947 Powderhall Sprint. This meant moving for about six week to Saltcoats in Ayrshire where he was told the air would be more beneficial to his training.

It paid off in more ways than one. He took the gold medal and £1,000 prize but made an absolute fortune in bets. It was with some of that cash, brought back to Blyth wrapped in a bed sheet, that Albert went on a three year course to qualify as a chiropodist and physiotherapist. After passing he opened a surgery in a small shop in Coomassie Road then moved it to his home in Bondicar Terrace.

Ten years later in 1957 another runner from Blyth, Joe Ball, who worked as a moulder at the Blyth Star Foundry and who was trained by Albert, also won the Powderhall title. After that race the team behind the bid gathered in the Portobella Hotel near the track in Joe's bedroom. I was there with Albert, Joe's father Sammy, a former goalkeeper for Blyth Spartans and Joe Barratt, who played saxophone in Tommy Bell's band at the Roxy Ballroom. It took us ages to count the winnings from the various bets which were strewn all over the bed.

Albert Grant who won the Powderhall Sprint championship running as W. Spence of Blyth.

Albert Grant (left) Gerry Evans (centre) and Joe Ball train on the ash track laid behind the west stand at Croft Park, the home of Blyth Spartans.

Shrewd gamblers, and we weren't bad at the game, would place bets at long odds before the start of racing, sometimes as high as 50-1. The bookies, however, would start to reduce the odds when a "prepped" runner – someone specially trained for the event – was spotted in the heats. The skill was in getting as much money on your runner before he was revealed.

Albert's full name was Albert Spencer Grant but it was a handicapper at one of the smaller events who called him Spence and gave him a Christian name of Walter which was shortened to Wally.

Albert was able to continue racing while studying and it was under his Wally Spence title that he embarked on a six months visit to Australia over 1949 and 1950 to compete in the professional world championship.

Down Under

Down Under he was known as the "White Ghost" because of the all white track suit with his initials on that he wore at every event. His visit Down Under proved worthwhile for he won not only the championship but also two other top events, the Stawell Invitation and the Wendouree Gift in the process beating Barney Ewell, the Olympic Games double silver medallist who had turned pro, and he did it a third time when Ewell came to England.

The fastest amateur runner in the world at that time was MacDonald Bailey and Tommy Potter challenged him to take on Albert over three winner take all races to be held in three venues in England. A telegram duly arrived from Bailey's agent asking for personal details including Albert's height and weight. This, while puzzling, was duly sent then a second telegram arrived requesting the same information. Some time later Bailey announced he had decided to keep his amateur status and would not turn professional. A year later he joined Leigh as a professional rugby league player.

On his return to Blyth from Australia Albert launched the Spence Training School of which I was a member and his advice and training certainly did me some good because I won races at Ambleside and Bridge of Aln worth £100 each, plus the gambling winnings, as well as handicaps in Blyth and Bedlington.

I ran under my real name because in 1948 a rule was introduced that runners could only race under their own name. Apparently some runners were appearing at one sprint under one name one day and then changing it the next day to compete in another race. This made life rather difficult for the handicappers who gave starts according to performances but certainly gave the runner a distinct advantage as far as betting was concerned. Fortunately W. Spence of Blyth still appeared on programmes as runners were allowed to keep the names they used before the ruling.

We trained in Croft Park on an ash running track behind the west stand. One of the runners who didn't train with us was Ivor McAnany who became British Professional Sprint Champion but two runners who came to Blyth to work with Albert and who both ran second at Powderhall were Bill Innes from Scotland and George Davies of Thorneyhaugh.

Son Carl

Another was Albert's son, Carl, who was educated in Edinburgh and at Blyth Grammar School, and who literally cleaned up as an amateur with national sprint titles at schoolboy and adult level. He eventually turned professional and finished second at Powderhall on one occasion but he was first in the prestigious Galashiels event. Following in his father's footsteps he toured the running tracks of Australia with a modicum of success. Carl also set up business as a chiropodist and masseur in Blyth where he still works.

Albert went on to form the Blyth Athletic Club which survived for a number of years using a track around a football pitch at 12th Avenue. He also took up organising races under the title of Spence Promotions for which I did the administrative work.

Those involved in professional or amateur athletics often ponder what would have

Albert Grant winning the 1947 Powderhall Sprint and making enough money to pay for a three year course in chiropody and physiotherapy.

Albert receiving his winners medal at the Powderhall sprint triumph.

happened if Albert hadn't taken money to run but the animosity of the amateur athletic authorities to professional runners was such that he was the subject of an article in The People national newspaper on June 27th, 1954.

It read: "While our athletes are on the way to Vancouver for the Empire Games, the fastest man in Britain over 100 yards languishes as the back marker in most handicaps and is utterly unable to get a race off scratch. Had Blyth's professional champion Albert Grant remained an amateur he would have been the toast of Britain today. He sacrificed that fame because he needed the money which came with turning professional."

While Albert's main love was running he was also a keen rider and trainer of event horses and greyhounds. He often boasted that he had beaten Harvey Smith at one gymkhana in a race. It turned out to be a novelty event where riders, after racing around the course, had to dismount and sprint in to the centre to touch a pole. Albert always said Harvey must have been unaware that that he had been a sprint champion.

Albert died of brain tumour at the age of 54 but his record has never been surpassed and is unlikely to be as there is no longer a professional world championship. W. Spence was unbeaten over 100 yards and is the only runner to appear in six Powderhall finals, coming second twice and third once. It was only the fact that the race officials did not want a runner to win their title twice that made it difficult to achieve because of their control over the start marks. Albert was always at the back. There is no doubt that had W. Spence of Blyth been allowed to run as an amateur he would have won at least one Olympic gold medal and possibly more.

He ran 100 yards on grass in 9.6 seconds. Who knows what time he would have achieved on today's tartan tracks?

Big Business for Blyth

It was in the Astley Arms, Seaton Sluice, one summer night in 1964 that Don Kent was approached by a man he vaguely recognized. After an exchange of pleasantries he was asked: "Do you want to buy the shipyard?" It was then the penny dropped. He was with the man whose job it was to liquidate the recently closed Blyth Dry Docks and Shipbuilding Company.

Don Kent was the general manager and secretary of the highly successful Blyth Harbour Commission which had already attracted many jobs to East Northumberland.

Don replied he was interested and his companion then said: "How much will you pay?" The reply was £4,000 to which the man replied: "For one dock?" His answer: "No, for the whole yard." Don didn't get it at that price but after a series of negotiations a price was agreed and the Commission took over the five dry docks, three slipways and acres of land.

"When the deal was signed I sat alone on the edge of one dry dock, looked around, and asked myself what I had done," he said. "I really didn't know how we were going to utilise everything but as it turned out it proved a very good deal."

Donald Kent was born on November 11th, 1919, in Sutton, Surrey, and joined the Port of London Authority in 1936 on the administrative side. A keen sportsman he

Don Kent in 1984.

played tennis, badminton and football and later became a soccer referee.

He was an active Rover Scout in his youth and also a member of the 5th London Corps of Signals in the Territorial Army. He tells how, in 1939, he spent two weeks at a Rover Scout camp in Scotland and returned to London in time to go off on another two weeks camp with the TA. By the time he came back the Second World War had started. This led to a commission as a lieutenant in the Signals Corps and he spent the entire war helping to maintain communications among the forces both home and abroad. He boasts of being one of the few officers in the war with electric windscreen wipers on his staff car – courtesy of the RAF for whom he often did jobs.

After War

His return to the Port of London Authority after the war in 1946 lasted only a year as he joined the Tees Conservancy Commission in Middlesbrough. It was on Teesside in 1949 he married his wife Mary, a marriage which lasted until her death in 2009. They had two sons, Martin and John.

It was while he was in Middlesbrough that he helped plan the building of the Tees Dock but did not see its completion as he moved to Blyth in 1956 as assistant to George Atkinson, the then general manager of the Harbour Commission.

He can recall his new boss taking him on a river tour shortly after he arrived and on approaching the new Blyth Power Station being asked: "How do you like coming to a dying port? That place is going to take all our coal and there won't be any for export." Some years later Don was in the top job himself and responsible for building Blyth into the largest coal exporting port in Europe shipping in 1961 a total of 6,891,317 tons. Even now, at 91, the figures proudly trip easily off his tongue along with: "The power station did not make much difference."

The five year plan he implemented to help expand the type of exports and imports at the port was proving highly successful, particularly the lucrative paper trade. He readily gives credit to two Blyth-born men for this – Mike Goonan, his commercial manager, and Eddie Ferguson, the owner of Fergusons Transport who readily provided the necessary vehicles.

Don's "What have I done?" comment on buying the shipyard was answered as the large sheds in the shipyard were ideal for storing the huge bales of paper until new ones could be built. Initially the carrying of the heavy bales was proving extremely difficult for the fork life trucks in the port which kept breaking down. A visit to a company in County Durham which imported a foreign built type of fork lift truck by Mike Goonan and works manager, Arnold Hopper, led to Blyth being the first port in Britain to use the Linde model which they had seen in action and proved ideal for the job.

As pits started to close there was a need to diversify and the port began to build up a trade in pit props, cement, tiles and a brand new export commodity – barley. An American had taken over a farm near Lynemouth and introduced new growing methods much to the displeasure of local farmers. He was so successful that the first shipment of the grain totalled over 4,000 tons and was brought to the docks in a fleet of lorries provided by Eddie Ferguson.

An aerial view of Blyth Harbour taken in the 1920's. Ritson's Shipyard can be seen to the top left of the picture where the Bates Terminal is now.

Another gigantic boost to the region came when rumours of a possible aluminium smelting plant for the area started to circulate. Don Kent was asked to take a mysterious man on a tour of land adjacent to the river.

"He never told me what he was after or which company he represented," said Don. "After the visit he actually left his notebook in my office which I forwarded on to him in London and no, I didn't look at it. It was only some months later I learned it was Alcan when I got a phone call from him when he arrived at Newcastle Central Station. He said they had decided to build the smelting plant at Lynemouth. This, of course, meant a tremendous boost for us as berths would have to be found for the ships, mainly from America, bringing in tons of aluminum. Another key factor was that there was already a mineral railway line from North Blyth running to Lynemouth.

Not only did the Alcan smelter provide hundred of jobs but a power station was needed and the company built Lynemouth Power Station in 1972 less than a thousand yards from the smelter which also helped the local unemployment situation.

By this time Blyth Harbour Commission had expanded greatly and owned nearly all the land along the river including the former Hughes Bolckow shipbreaking yard. This gave great scope for developments including berths for shipping although it would mean changes in the river itself. It needed to be deepened to take the Alcan ships bringing in the aluminium and this led to a furore in the town.

Don says: "The problem we faced was that sand on Blyth beach was being brought into the river by the tides causing a build up. This would have to be cleared regularly. Our bucket dredger, the *Cowpen*, was not suitable for the job and we sold it to an Italian company and bought the suction dredger the *Crofton*. In order to assist we then gave Lance Wood, a well known Blyth business man, the rights to remove sand from the beach to help us in keeping the river clear.

The bucket dredger, the 'Cowpen'.

"When it was realised the sand was being taken and that the beach was being deprived there were stories in the papers and letters of protest. I was called in front of the full Blyth Borough Council to explain why it was happening and fortunately the council accepted my explanation and the protests died down."

Another decision which caused some protests was when the Harbour Commission decided to withdraw the 100-year-old chain ferry between north and south Blyth in 1962. The ferry, which could carry cars as well as passengers, was badly affected by the opening of the Kitty Brewster bridge at Bebside.

Don said: "The easier road access to Cambois and the other side of the river made the ferry uneconomical. There were protests – as it was one of the features of the town but times change – but not as many as over the sand removal."

Don Kent was easily recognisable in the town as he was the only person who wore a bowler hat. He didn't have one when he arrived in Blyth but explained it had all come about because of a visit to the North East by Lord Hailsham, the Minister of Transport, in 1963.

He said: "It got out that his Lordship had bought himself a cloth cap for his visit to the region and this brought about howls of protest and claims that he was lowering the tone. I decided to have my own little protest by buying and wearing a bowler during his visit to Blyth and our sail up the river on the tug *Chipchase* and I continued wearing it after he left."

Lord Hailsham (wearing a cap) and Don Kent (wearing a bowler).

The tug, which had been launched in 1953, did not need Lord Hailsham to grab the headlines on July 8th, 1964, when it sank in the river while towing the 712 ton collier, *Blackwall Point*, into dry dock. The collier was moving upstream under power when the tug was pulled over. With the docks awash the crew of five only had seconds to escape before the tow rope snapped and the tug sank.

According to the Blyth News, David Carter the 20-year-old deckhand, of Bath Terrace, swam fifty yards to safety while fireman Daniel McBain, aged 48, of Nixon Terrace was pulled from the water by Gladstone Hardy, a ship's chandler. The remaining members of the crew, Jack Barrett, the 40-year-old skipper of Avondale Road, Bebside, Robert Bell, the 30-year-old engineer of Haughton Terrace and Frank Mullen, the mate, of South Newsham, were picked up by a foyboatman, Fred Simpson. All the crew were taken to the Thomas Knight Memorial Hospital in Beaconsfield Street and after being checked over were allowed home.

The *Chipchase* remained on the bottom of the Blyth for nineteen days while Don Kent endeavoured to get a lifting vessel in to the port but it was soon back at work. The tug was sold to Seaham Harbour four years later. In 1993 it was in the Maryport Maritime Museum but lack of funds for maintenance led to it being broken up at Millom in Cumbria in 1998.

Retirement came for Don Kent in 1984, two years after he received the OBE from the Queen Mother at Buckingham Palace for services to the port industry.

"I was very proud to receive the honour as I have always been a supporter of the British Empire," he said. "My wife Mary was there with me and it was a lovely occasion for both of us."

He left the Harbour Commission with regret. "Retirement was compulsory at 65," he said. "It would have been nice to continue as I loved the town and the job but it was not to be."

From his bungalow home in Whitley Bay he looks back on his 55 years in Blyth with great pleasure although his health has not been of the best recently. He has had hip and knee replacements and his left leg amputated but he is able to get around on an artificial limb, drive his car and still, on occasions, visit Blyth Rotary Club at the Spartan Hotel of which he is a past president.

Above: The funnel and part of the superstructure are all that is visible of the sunken 'Chipchase' which lay on the bottom of the river for 19 days until the right type of lifting gear was brought to the river.

Right: Four years after being repaired and refurbished in dry dock the 'Chipchase' was sold to Seaham Harbour. It was eventually broken up at Millom in Cumbria in 1998 after efforts to preserve it failed because of lack of funds.

The Donkey at the Roxy

George Downey is believed to have the unique record of being the only man in Blyth to have served in the Royal Navy, the Merchant Navy and the Royal Air Force during the Second World War. In the navy he watched one of his colleagues getting a punishment lashing and as a rear gunner survived an air crash which killed two of the crewmates. He was also responsible for taking a donkey in to a dance at the Roxy Ballroom!

George Downey is an extremely colourful character as you are to find out. He was born on January 31st, 1923, in Phoenix Street, Newsham, to George, a miner, and Mary Ann. Soon after starting Newsham Infants School he found himself on a boat for Canada with his family after his mother had persuaded her reluctant husband to join her relatives in the mining industry in Newcastletown. After a year they were on the move again this time to the United States and again to relatives of his mother where his father resumed his mining career in Homestead, Pennsylvania.

George snr still hankered after Newsham and eventually persuaded Mary Ann to make the move. Although their American relatives wanted young George to stay the whole family returned to England.

George said: "We had no place to live when we came back and the family was broken up. Dad went to live with relatives in the Isabella while my mother, me and my sister, moved in with her mother in Ridley Street, down by the Quayside, which was quite an unpleasant place to be in those days because of certain bad characters and nasty families. Although the split was supposed to be temporary we never came together again."

George Downey.

Blyth Yank

The move meant George attended the nearby Plessey Road Infants School where he was called the "Blyth Yank" because of his American accent and clothes. He had attended school over there and was still wearing knickerbockers – the standard dress for boys over the Atlantic.

He soon settled into his new life and one of his pastimes was fishing from the Quayside with other youngsters. He says: "We used bent pins and string to catch little crabs and fish and just threw them back. However, an old woman called Mrs Birt, who lived nearby, told us to take everything we caught to her. The first time we did she threw everything into a big cast iron pot which was bubbling on the fire. The next time we went she gave us a big mug of broth from the pot. It was delicious and we became regular visitors to her home after that."

George tells of how families who lived in the Quayside were called the River People and others in other parts of the town – the Crofton People, the Cowpen People, the Bella People etc – and we all looked down on each other."

He remembers his visits to the Hippodrome cinema near the bus station and watched the Wallaw being built in Union Street in 1937. "The Hippodrome had a corrugated iron roof and everyone prayed that it didn't rain during the picture because you couldn't hear the sound."

From Plessey Infants George went on to Princess Louise Road Senior School where he stayed until he was 14 when he left to start work at the Crofton Mill Pit.

"I didn't like it so a week after my 15th birthday in 1938 I was old enough to join the Boys' Navy, which had been formed to attract boys to a life at sea, and soon found myself on HMS *Caledonia* at Rosyth in Scotland. It had been a luxury liner which had been used by the Germans during the First World War and was now a training vessel for us in the Boys' Navy. One of my most vivid memories was seeing a boy flogged. He was a Cockney and one of the strict rules on board was that smoking was not allowed until you were eighteen.

"This lad used to go into Rosyth and buy those paper packets of five Woodbines. He would bring them back to the ship and sell them to other lads. As we didn't have any matches, which were banned, he found an ingenious way of using two lead pencils and a piece of flammable wadding to short circuit the light switch in the cabin and produce a spark from which one cigarette was lit which serviced all the others.

"Anyhow he was brought before the CO on a charge. Now in those days the punishment rules from the time of Nelson still applied, including the lash which had been replaced by the cane, and he was given the option of six strokes or two weeks confinement on board. As it was almost time for Easter leave and he wanted to go to London to see his family the lad opted for the caning.

"We were all lined up on deck and he was brought forward. He was allowed to wear his canvas duck suit, which we all wore when working, and told to bend forward. The Chief Petty Officer administered the first stroke on top of the suit which produced a yelp from the lad, and then stepped back. Our medical officer then pulled down the trousers to see if the blow had drawn blood. Had the blow broken the skin then the punishment would have been stopped.

There was a red wheal but no blood and the lad got five more strokes. His backside was all the colours of the rainbow.

"A couple of days later we were all off on leave on the train from Rosyth. He stood all the way to Newcastle and I was told that he did not sit down at all travelling on to London."

George Downey in Navy uniform.

Boys Drowned

At the outbreak of war in 1939 George found himself posted to HMS *Chatham* but his stay in the Royal Navy was coming to an end following the sinking of the *Royal Oak* battleship in Scapa Flow by a German submarine. A large number of youngsters in the Boys' Navy had been drowned on the ship and there was quite a row in Parliament about the deaths.

"My mother kicked up quite a fuss and wrote to the War Ministry and I was discharged on compassionate grounds when I was seventeen years and four months old as it was then ruled no-one under the age of eighteen could join the Royal Navy."

George went back to Crofton Pit but in 1941 switched careers again by joining the Merchant Navy where he sailed from Blyth on colliers running coal to power stations in the south of England.

He said: "I must have sailed on every collier out of Blyth as I was attached to what was called the Relieving Pool on the Quayside. I took the place of any member of the crew who was taking leave. You were entitled to a week's leave for every six months worked."

By this time George was a regular at the Roxy Ballroom with the "Seghini Gang" – a group of friends who met in Seghini's café on Waterloo Road which in those days backed on to the Alexandra Billiard Hall. His gang included Jacky Allen, Stan Williamson, Terry Morgan and Vic Tuff and there they supped hot blackcurrant juice from a very restricted menu.

At the time George was still sailing on the colliers and his friends would assemble on the Quayside to wave him off before they went on to the Roxy. One night after such a farewell he astonished his mates when he turned up. Apparently two relief crew had been sent in mistake and George persuaded the pilot to take him back to shore with him.

The Seghini gang also enjoyed beer when they could get it. Ale was in extremely short supply and there were limited deliveries to the pubs in the town.

George recalls: "I heard that the Commercial, which was where Greggs the Bakers is now, had got a supply and I went over. Now not only was beer in short supply those days but glasses were as well. What you had to do was stand at the bar and wait until someone had finished with his glass. On this occasion I was next in line for a glass and just as it was about to be handed over to me this lad I knew grabbed it and disappeared out of the bar.

"I didn't manage to get another glass and so didn't get a pint. Later that night when I was dancing in the Roxy I saw the lad near me so I told him I wanted to see him. When the dance finished I met him next to the band stand when I took him up for stealing the glass. He had apparently used it to get beer in the bottle and jug end, and the argument ended when I hit him and he fell to the floor. He got up and I hit him again. When he got up this time he said: "Geordie, you hit too ... hard!"

George didn't get banned from the Roxy on that occasion but he did on another. He explains: "It was a terribly hot night and we were all sweltering in the ballroom. I spotted the emergency doors near the bandstand and decided to open them. The rush of air was marvellous and people started standing next to me to cool down. I noticed a donkey was grazing on the open land just a few yards away so I took it by the halter and trotted it into the ballroom.

"Tommy Bell, the bandleader, saw what was happening and immediately struck up *Donkey Serenade.* Everyone was falling about laughing, except the Master of Ceremonies, Ralph Halligan. He dashed across and on seeing part of the dance floor had been

Tommy Bell and his Band. Back row: Norman Snowden (bass) Dennis Hutchinson (drums). Front row: Tommy Bell, Charlie Woollens (trombone), Stevie Hogg and Mattie Davison (trumpets), Norman Waddle (violin & saxophone), John Gurney (sax) and Johnny Adams (sax).

damaged by the shoes on the donkey barred me from the ballroom."

It was in 1943 that George changed careers once more and joined the Royal Air Force as an air gunner where he linked up again with Vic Tuff, one of the Seghini mob, when they spent a week receiving their physicals and "jabs" at the Lords Cricket Ground. George was posted to Tranwell Aerodrome near Morpeth and it was soon after he arrived there that the donkey incident occurred. Sammy Williamson, who lived in Cowpen, had loaned him a bicycle so he could cycle from Tranwell to see his mother and also to meet his mates at the Roxy. He would then pedal back to Morpeth in the early hours.

"Actually because of my training I wasn't at the Roxy as often as I liked but when I did return I found my ban for the donkey incident had been forgotten," he said.

Air training at Tranwell was in Anson aircraft and many a time he flew over Blyth to practice firing at targets towed by other planes over the sea. "We used bullets painted in different colours so we could see how many times we hit the target as they left a mark," he said. He eventually joined the crew of a Wellington bomber at the air base at Chipping Norton near Banbury.

It was there that his flying career came to a sudden end. During a night flying exercise his pilot, Bob Crabtree, an Australian, sent out a Mayday call when one of the engines cut out at 11,800 feet.

"I knew exactly how high we were because I heard him giving the height to a aircraftswoman in the operations room on the ground. It was terrifying as we lost height in the darkness. Bob was having to keep our only engine at top revs to stay in the air. We eventually made the runway and then Bob had to raise our undercarriage to slow us down when we belly landed.

"I was in the rear gunner's cockpit and was knocked unconscious by the bouncing as we skidded along. I was lucky, two of the crew

George in RAF uniform.

were killed when the plane broke up. I was treated for concussion and never flew again."

The year 1945 saw George back at Crofton Pit as a face worker and later he moved to the surface to become an NCB driver.

The eventful life of George Downey settled down somewhat in 1947 when he married Nancy Raisbeck, daughter of the owner of the Raisbeck Coaches firm in Bedlington, whom he had met at the Roxy. He later passed his PSV test and did some part time coach driving for her father. Nancy and George eventually raised a family of two sons, Peter and Michael and a daughter Susan.

It is the mention of Michael which brings sadness to the normally smiling George as his son, who was a marine engineer on liners, disappeared in 1970 while in Australia and despite extensive searches by the family, including appeals on Aussie television, radio and in newspapers, nothing has been heard of him.

George, at 87, now lives alone in a bungalow in Broomlinn Place, Cramlington, but is mobile enough to visit his home town every day where he links up and yarns with the surviving members of the Seghini Gang.

The frontage of the Roxy Ballroom has changed over the years mainly through repainting jobs and the removal of the huge Roxy sign. The double door behind George was the main entrance to the ballroom which, following a forty yards walk, led into the actual dance floor area which was situated in the brick building to the extreme right. The field where the donkey was kept has long disappeared and is a concreted area now.

Tanks & the T & B Garage

Peter Thompson was born on January 30th, 1926, the son of Ronald, a solicitor in Blyth, and Lilian, and spent his early years at 16 Crown Street. He was educated at Plessey Road Junior School and Blyth Secondary School, and, courtesy of the Army, at Sunderland Technical College. He was later to head the T. & B. Garage company which was the first in the town to run holiday coaches around Britain and Europe.

Peter writes:

My father, who was a solicitor in Blyth at the turn of the century, was also joint founder of the T. & B. Garage in Post Office Square. He had served in the First World War, beginning as a despatch rider in the Northern Cyclists unit and later as a lieutenant in the Welsh Fusiliers. It was while serving in the infantry he was severely gassed.

Peter Thompson.

In 1919 he was invalided out of the army and went into partnership with a man called Billy Bowman to open the Thompson and Bowman garage – believed to be the first in the town, alongside the old Theatre Royal and opposite the old Hippodrome cinema where the Roxy bingo hall now stands.

Apart from the T. & B. Garage, his law practice, a busy one as in those days a law firm had one solicitor and a clerk, Dad was also secretary of the Blyth Conservative Club in Croft Road.

While keeping active he never fully recovered from that wartime gassing and eventually died in 1942 when I was sixteen and so too young to really get to know him. His death halted what might have led me into a career in law. Dad had arranged, subject to my getting exam credits in Latin, English and Maths, to become an articled clerk with a law firm in Newcastle. I got the requisite passes but after his death I heard nothing more.

My education continued at the Secondary School until I was seventeen and on that day I got my driving licence. Almost around the same time I spotted an advertisement offering training in engineering at Sunderland Technical College on condition you joined the Army on completion of the one year course. Now having joined the Home Guard in Blyth, which was being run by Nigel Parry our school headmaster, I had some semblance of military training.

The showroom of the T. & B. Garage in Post Office Square fronting the garage area which stretched from behind the showroom up to and almost against the Theatre Royal. To the right of the picture are the offices used by staff at the Blyth Coke and Gasworks. They were eventually pulled down along with the garage and the theatre to make room for the Keel Row Shopping Mall and car park.

In 1928 the staff of the T. & B. Garage had an outing to Allendale in one of the company's coaches, naturally. The young boy in the front row is the author of this article, Peter Thompson who is being held by his grandmother, while his father is the 'Mr' on the back row. Back row, left to right: Bob Stephenson, G. Todd, G. Mason, J. Hepple, N. Anderson, Ted Turpin, Mr R.W. Thompson. Second row: Jim Gledson, Miss Bell, Elsie Thompson, Mary Hogarth, Betty Weir, Thora Davison. Front row: Mrs Bell, Grandma Thompson, Peter Thompson, Basil Stephenson, a Blyth freelance journalist who took the picture using a length of string, Betty Turpin, Maggie Hodgson and Zena Foster.

The headquarters of the Home Guard was in the huge, detached, Presbyterian Manse in Cypress Gardens. It later became the nurses home for the Beulah House maternity hospital and when it closed was eventually taken over by Eddie Ferguson, head of Ferguson's Transport, who was killed with his youngest son, Stuart, in a tragic helicopter crash on December 6th, 1989.

It was there in the grounds that a motley gathering of men and boys of all ages gathered to train. We had rifles but no ammunition and I am still waiting to fire my first shot. Our commanding officer was none other than my secondary school headmaster, Nigel Parry, but by this time, 1943, the threat of invasion having subsided, the Home Guard was being kept on – just in case.

The manse now belongs to a retired doctor but the surface tunnel connecting Beulah House maternity hospital to the Manse being used as the nurses home – has long gone.

It wasn't the Home Guard square bashing that attracted me to the Army advert but the fact I was to be trained as an engineer. I jumped at the chance even though it meant having to lodge in Sunderland throughout the week getting home only at the weekends via the Economic and United bus services and the North Shields ferry.

My career in the army which lasted three years began in 1945 after I finished at Sunderland when I was posted to the Royal Electrical and Mechanical Engineers in Pocklington, North Yorkshire, for training and afterwards to Germany where we carried out maintenance on vehicles in our various depots. One bonus was that I was given the opportunity of driving tanks – a fascinating experience, albeit a wet one when testing in water as there was no cover on the driver's vision hatch.

One day I was called into the Commanding Officer's room and told I had been selected for officer training in the Infantry. At the time I was a corporal but I turned it down as I wanted to continue learning car mechanics as I had then decided I wanted to join the family firm, now solely owned by the Thompson family, as the original partnership had been dissolved in 1938.

The T & B fleet of luxury touring coaches were garaged on the company's Maddison Street site. The fleet eventually numbered eighteen and carried thousands of passengers over the years on trips around Britain and Europe.

After father's death the garage was kept going through the efforts Margaret Kirk, who ran the office. She had started as a girl in 1928 and spent 75 years with the company until she died on December 13th, 2009, at the age of 97. She had her hands full in those wartime years as the Army was forever commandeering our vehicles for the war effort – I think we lost twelve in all. We didn't get them back either. There was also a shortage of drivers as several of ours were called up and she was a godsend in helping to keep the business going after my father died in 1942.

The mechanical side of the business was in the hands of Bob Stephenson who, during the war, was exempt from the forces as he was making tanks at the Vickers Armstrong works in Newcastle during the day and then spending the night in the garage repairing the vehicles. Another who kept it going for a short while before serving in the army where he saw combat as a Desert Rat was George Hudson. He was later to suffer an horrific accident when coming to the aid of a stricken motor cyclist.

George was driving a coach on Waterloo Road when he saw a motor cycle on fire. He stopped and grabbed the bus fire extinguisher. As he was putting out the flames the petrol tank exploded and George suffered severe burns to his face and hands. He spent a year away from work recovering but returned to continue as a most valued member of our team. He was with us for nearly 50 years as was Bob Stephenson and his son, Alan.

The Roxy Ballroom and the Post Office Square were dominated by the huge structure of the now vanished Blyth Coke works. The square was later redesigned losing much of its character – the centre piece and the flower beds included.

The 1950's saw a big change in Blyth with the building of the new Bus Station in Post Office Square. I can remember some workmen employed on the job asking why their excavations were always flooding. We had to point out to them that they were close to a river which ran underneath Waterloo Road, locals called it the Flanker although I don't know why, and high tides always caused flooding. We had an example of this ourselves when we had a repair pit built in the garage and after it was flooded the Morpeth firm which had put it in were able to make it flood proof. Anyhow the bus station was eventually built on a huge raft and this did the trick. Even so the Waterloo Road junction with Regent Street continued to flood until a large drain was put in down the full length of Marine Terrace in the 1960's.

In 1900 an extremely high Spring tide and easterly wind wreaked havoc in the centre of Blyth with flooding affecting scores of shops. This picture was taken the day after it occurred when it was possible to wade in the streets. Twenty four hours earlier it was deep enough to swim in.

It was in that same period that Sol Sheckman, who owned the Essoldo and the Roxy Ballroom in the town, called as he was visiting the area and asked if I wanted to buy the Theatre Royal. Whether he was serious or not I don't know but the offer was politely declined.

It was in 1951 I decided to branch out into luxury coaches – the first such company in the town. Harold Blakeborough, who was also a first – the first travel agent in Blyth, would organise holidays and trips away from the town and business began to boom. We took parties to Solingen in Germany, which is Blyth's twin town, on a number of occasions and eventually we were running eighteen luxury coaches all over Europe and Britain, where holiday camps were a very popular destinations.

Business took a bit of a back seat in 1956 with my marriage to Mary Fordyce, daughter of Harry Fordyce, who had arrived from Scotland to set up a chemists business in the town. Mary, who was known as Queenie, derived from the Scot's name "Quiny", was a teacher who worked at Crofton and Princess Louise schools. She took a break from teaching when son Peter arrived in 1965 but returned to the classroom for a few more years.

As far as T. & B. was concerned in those days we sold new cars but had to buy them from the big firms in Newcastle who held the franchise. Sometimes they would refuse to sell, as was their right, but when they did it meant we only had a month to pay for them which meant a lot of capital was tied up.

Eventually we got the Vauxhall franchise for the Blyth area and it went well for a time but the company started pushing us to expand to make provision for a larger showroom.

It had already taken us almost seven years to get planning permission to rebuild the garage and on this occasion, while we were able to buy up some of the surrounding properties, we suddenly found ourselves facing the massive Keel Row shopping mall plan. As David Crawford, the Chief Planning Officer for Blyth, said when I asked him what was happening: "Peter, you'll be the last to know." He was referring, although he did not say so, to prolonged discussions on the sale of other properties, including the Grade Two listed building, the Central Methodist Church, on which the whole plan rested.

I began looking around for another site and settled on developing the Maddison Street premises we owned and where the coaches were kept. We bought the old Electricity Board building which had been standing empty for over a year and the small Gatacre Street alongside. We had already given up the Vauxhall franchise before we moved and while all the staff of 30 wanted to stay on it was with a lot of sorrow we had to make nine redundant. Part of that site is now where the Waterloo Health Centre is situated.

The levelling of the garage, the church and the other places near Post Office Square to make way for the Mall in the early 90's was also a sad occasion and an offer for our business from the Chambers Car Sales in 1981 led to my eventual retirement at the age of seventy five.

While my work in the company took an awful lot of my time I was still able to give active support to Blyth Rotary Club in which I completed 50 years in 2006, and the Blyth Round Table, of which I was chairman in 1956 helping to organise our popular annual Blyth Carnival which was the biggest charity event held in the town. It is with some regret that it no longer takes place because of a lack of interest by local organisations in providing floats for the parade.

The complete management team of the T. & B. Garage pose outside the showrooms in Post Office Square. From left to right: George Hudson, Bob Stephenson, Peter Thompson, Margaret Kirk and Alan Stephenson.

The £6,500 Newsham Pigeon

Jim Derbyshire was born on December 3rd, 1934, at 6 Single Row, South Newsham, and attended Newsham Infants School and New Delaval Senior School leaving at the age of 15 to start work as an assistant greenkeeper at Blyth Golf Club. He left after only six months to begin a career in the mines as a face worker which was to last 36 years. Throughout all that time Jim's consuming passion has been racing pigeons. This is his story.

I got my first pigeon when I was twelve but I didn't really take it up seriously until I was sixteen when I got my first loft on the allotments behind the Newsham and New Delaval Social Club and where I still have my birds.

I suppose you can say I used the hobby to enjoy the fresh air after working down the pit. My first underground shift was at the Seaton Delaval drift mine and when it closed I transferred to Bates Pit in Blyth where I stayed until my early retirement in 1985. It was shortly after the long miners' strike, which was led locally by our union men, Ronnie Campbell, now MP for Blyth and Alec Turner, which had an effect on my family.

My son Jimmy lived at home and was at Bates. He had gone back to work two weeks before the strike ended along with some of his young mates who were penniless. They were then labelled scabs. I wasn't affected as I was on maintenance then making sure the pit could run on the return to work.

After the strike the management announced that men over 55

Jim Derbyshire at his loft.

could apply for redundancy as a guarantee that the jobs of the younger lads would be protected. I agreed for Jimmy's sake. The promise, as we all know, was not kept and the pit closed within two years with the men transferred to other pits. Unfortunately men at those collieries continued to regard Jimmy and the others as scabs so he finished and went into factory work.

Jimmy hasn't gone in for pigeon racing, which at one time was purely a pitman's sport, but I couldn't and wouldn't be without it. Over the years I must have trained hundreds of birds, yes trained. People who don't know about pigeons ask how you can train a bird. It's not just a question of putting them in boxes and sending them to faraway places and letting them fly home.

Like any athlete they have to be looked after and cosseted, fed on the best corn and subject to discipline and routine. The racing season is over the summer but the rest of the year my racers are allowed out of their lofts twice a day at certain times and there is strict segregation.

We pair the cocks and hens up the second week in January to allow them to mate and then separate them, not allowing them to mix unless we want them or race. Each hen lays two eggs which hatch within eighteen days. The chicks are removed after 28 days and put in their own cree.

On my allotment I have two lofts divided into two sections each. The young cocks and the young hens have their own individual sections as have the older ones. There is method in this for like any creature the birds have the urge to mate and this is an advantage when racing. Say if there's a race on a Saturday you introduce your racer to his paired hen on Friday where they do what they have to do for ten minutes. They're then returned to their cree until they're collected to be transported to the start point. It's a fact that when they are released they increase their speed to get back to their hen and indulge in a further session of lovemaking. This lasts another ten minutes and then they're taken away again until the next Friday when the session is repeated. This system is called Widowhood, why? I don't know but it's used throughout the pigeon world.

In the south the pigeon races sometimes have cars and big cash for prizes sometimes as much as £10,000 for the winner but up here in the Up North Combine the prizes are much smaller, sometimes a thousand, but not very big. It doesn't mean you cannot win big cash here as I made an awful lot of money in 2002.

I put my best bird, Derbys Girl, in for the biggest race of the season, the Queen's Cup which starts in France. She was up against 17,143 other birds. Mine was the fastest home flying 431 miles and there was a heck of a lot of interest in her from breeders after that, including some from abroad. I eventually sold her for £6,500 to a man in Thailand and the money gave me the chance to build two new lofts.

Keith, Jim's son, in the mask he wears while inside the pigeon crees.

When I started 60 years ago the return of the birds during races was registered on the pigeon clocks with the ring being placed in the clock and then you ran the clocks to where times were being registered. We're now in the computer age for as soon as the bird lands and walks through the small door into the loft a chip on its leg activates the beam over the entrance registering the time of arrival.

My day starts every morning of the week, including weekends, at half past six when I go to the lofts and feed and let the birds out for their morning flight. There's ample time to indulge my other hobby, vegetable growing, while I await their return. I'm on duty until one o'clock in the afternoon when my son Keith, takes over. He flies them again in the afternoon and stays on duty until early evening. Mind you he has to wear a full headed mask when inside the lofts because he caught Pigeon Flu some time ago caused by a dust off the wings of the bird and it badly affected his chest for over a year. He's got rid of it now but always wears the mask when inside the crees.

My partner, Norma, is also keen on the birds and apart from taking them away to release them on training runs and doing stints at the allotment, not the digging mind you, she does grow better tomatoes than me, she also looks after the young ones. Actually I'm lucky that Keith, who's now 40, has taken up the pigeons because it is a dying sport. At one time it was traditional for the sons of the miners who kept the birds to take up the hobby but that is falling off.

Jim, Norma and Keith.

I'm a member of the Newsham Homing Society which has its headquarters in the Newsham and New Delaval Social Club where we meet on Friday nights. Ten years ago we had 39 members now we're down to 15 and one of them doesn't race his birds. We're trying to get youngsters interested by having open nights and showing off the birds, in fact we've given birds to youngsters and places to keep them but after about a year they give up – other things seem to interest them more.

The end of the season is decision time. By then we've probably 120 birds in the loft and we have to decide which ones to keep and which ones have to be culled to reduce costs by half.

People ask why we don't sell the pigeons for food but there doesn't appear to be any interest. On the other hand an Indian restaurant was prepared to take them but they wanted live birds and not carcasses. As we couldn't guarantee what treatment they would receive we decided it was more humane to dispose of them ourselves.

Our races are started in other parts of the country and in France while the start of the South Combine races can be seen in the summer in car parks in Whitley Bay, Berwick and Morpeth.

I often drive to Whitley Bay to watch the release from four carriers. The whole sky is filled with 10,000 birds like a swarm of starlings as the handles on vehicles, are pulled at the blowing of a whistle.

I don't think there's a more finer sight, of course I'm slightly biased!

The Dentist Bomb Aimer

Francis Armstrong was born on March 2nd, 1928, in Whitley Bay the son of Francis John and Ella. His father was a long serving police officer who later became chief constable of Northumberland and eventually one of only four H.M. Inspectors of Constabulary. Francis jnr was educated at schools in Whitley Bay, Bedlington and Morpeth then at the Dental School in Newcastle, part of Durham University, where he qualified as Bachelor of Dental Surgery. He settled in Blyth in 1955 and served on the British Dental Association for more than 20 years and is one of four life vice presidents. In 1981 he was invested with an Honorary Degree of Master of Dental Surgery by Newcastle University and holds several other university associated honours in dentistry. This is his story.

After qualifying as a dentist and being liable for two years National Service I volunteered for a four year short service commission in the RAF, entering with the rank of Flying Officer, not to take to the air but to provide dental care for my fellow servicemen very much on the ground.

It was that career in uniform, however, which took me to Malaya, Ceylon and Singapore. In Malaya, at that time, the communist insurgents had killed the Governor General and were continuing to attack from the jungle where the army was heavily engaged. Although I should have been confined to my dental work I was, on one occasion, invited by an Australian aircrew, who were on their last three weeks in their tour of duty, to go with them on a bombing mission. It was a thank you for the dental treatment I had given them.

Anyhow they put me in the front nose cone where the bomb release mechanism was and it was only when we were in the air I was told I was the bomb aimer and to drop my bombs into the jungle. The pilot told me these raids were requested by the army who, although they were ignorant of the precise location of any of the terrorist camps, had found this frightening type of bombing to be most effective in getting the enemy to surrender.

Once we were over the area to be bombed I pressed the button when ordered and watched the missiles sail down into the jungle. I hadn't been warned, possibly deliberately by the Aussies, that even at that height shock waves from the bomb blasts could reach the aircraft and give your stomach quite a jolt.

Francis Armstrong.

It was an interesting and fascinating sight watching the bombs actually explode and seeing the pressure waves opening up like giant flowers over the jungle foliage.

On another occasion I found myself on a train packed with soldiers and airmen heading for Kuala Lumpur. We were stationary for a while and eventually a sergeant major came up to me and said: "Permission for the train to move." I was rather taken aback but realised I was the senior officer on board so I gave the said permission much to the hidden amusement of the airmen who knew I was a non combatant.

My one regret when I was in the RAF was that I was not able to see my father, who was by this time one of the four Inspectors of Constabulary in the country, meet the Queen during the 1953 Coronation Parade in London. He was to shake hands with Her Majestry again this time in Buckingham Palace when he received his CBE from her for his police service.

On my demobilisation from the forces I was placed on the Reserve and later promoted to Squadron Leader but alas I never got to use my new found rank.

At the end of my active service in the RAF I advertised in the British Dental Journal for an appointment as a dentist and one of the replies brought me to Blyth and the post of assistant with Clark and McPherson in Beaconsfield Street. That partnership broke up just over a year later and although I was offered a job to stay on with Bill Clark I decided to branch out on my own.

In 1956, helped by a loan from my father and my own savings I bought 42 Marine Terrace, an end terraced house, which was to figure in my personal and working life for the next 37 years.

Frank's father meeting the Queen when he received his CBE from her for his police service.

Before moving in I employed Bob Bell, a well known Blyth decorator, to do what was necessary in the house to put it in good order. It had been built by a builder as his family home over a century earlier. Bob found it had up to twelve layers of wallpaper and he literally shuddered at my request to have them all removed as he was afraid the wall plaster would disintegrate.

When he got down to the second last paper he found written on the top right hand corner of a wall on the landing, in very small letters, the name of the decorator who had put the paper on and the date, April 4th, 1864. The date was just two days after the house had been sold by the builder to a Mr and Mrs Joseph Lee.

The biggest shock for both Bob and me was to come when the last paper, which had been heavily varnished, came off and we discovered a plaster which looked like polished marble. Neither Bob nor I had ever seen the like then or since. It was exquisite craftsmanship.

Mr Lee was a draper in the town and his wife a graduate schoolteacher – most unusual in those days. She used to tell how she could look out of her washhouse door, which faced on to Coomassie Road, over open fields to the North Farm such was the lack of housing and shop development in those days. Bear in mind the house in Marine Terrace was and is only a couple of hundred yards from Blyth Market Place.

In 1958 I married my wife Dorothy who started her teaching career at the Newminster and Chantry Schools in Morpeth and, on coming to Blyth, taught at three middle schools, Newsham and Princess Louise ending her teaching career at Delaval in Plessey Road.

Our first home was the flat on the first and second floors above the surgery and it was the family home for the next four years. It was there the first of our three sons, Francis John, spent his early years. In 1962 we bought a house in Middleton Street, just around the corner from the surgery, where Dorothy and I still live.

Other dental surgeons in Blyth at the time were Mr Stokes Brady in Waterloo Road, Messrs Jimmy Hughes, Bill Clark and Gerald Dale, all in Beaconsfield Street, and Mr. Bedgood in Stanley Street. I knew Gerald well as we were friends at King Edward VI School at Morpeth and at Dental School.

Prior to 1921 anyone could practice as a dentist but in that year it was enacted that those who had been practising for three years or more (and remember barbers with their red and white striped poles were still dealing with dental problems) could call themselves "Dentist" and were put on a Dental Register. Only those who qualified at university or Royal College were titled to call themselves dental surgeon. Even so after that time there were still men who practised unregistered. In Blyth there was one particular man who went around extracting teeth in pubs, clubs and peoples homes. He also used a first floor room above Donkin's newspaper shop in Havelock Street as a "surgery" where patients sat in a deep armchair for treatment.

The introduction of the 1948 Health Service Act with free dental treatment reduced the number of unregistered "freelances".

It had long been traditional, particularly in some mining areas, for people to have all their teeth removed and be fitted with dentures. I'm told sometimes a set of false teeth were often given to girls as a 21st birthday or pre-wedding present from grandparents.

As far as the brides were concerned this would save the husbands from having to pay for any future dental

Frank and his wife Dorothy.

treatment for their wives. The fitting of dentures wasn't because all the teeth were necessarily rotten but because dental hygiene was nil and gum disease was chronic most frequently through lack of brushing.

When I started my own practice one young man came in and I found he needed a few fillings. He said he didn't want fillings but wanted all his teeth out. He was most peeked and stormed out in high dudgeon when I refused to do what he asked. Whether he got them all removed elsewhere I do not know but he was not alone as quite a number of his contemporaries weren't interested in saving their teeth either and probably succeeded in having them all removed eventually.

My first patient when I opened on my own in 1956 was a Miss Joyce Minnear and I was delighted to welcome her. She was the only one that day but it was not long before I was being kept fully occupied. Another "first" then was a young girl, Maureen Cooper, who was my first receptionist/secretary. With only a short absence for child bearing following her marriage to Gordon Badenoch, a local police constable, she was with me as a senior staff member right up to my retirement. Maureen was quite incredible, apart from correcting forms I had completed, she could rattle off patients addresses on just being given a name. She continued with my successor until her retirement, which I hope is proving to be an enjoyable one.

In the early days of the health service all treatment was free but charges were eventually introduced, although never admitted by the Government, because of the widespread and costly abuse of the system. Some people, it was discovered, were visiting several dentists, getting new dentures free from each and then picking what they regarded as the best and throwing the others away.

In those days I received from the NHS 7s 6d, that's about 37 pence in today's money, for an extraction, 10s 6d for a filling and about £8 40p for dentures. Under the new regulations, which caused Aneurin Bevan, the architect of the National Health Service to resign from the government, patients had to pay the first £1 10s (£1 50p) of any treatment other than new dentures for which a charge of almost half the cost was levied. This was unless you were on National Assistance when they were supplied free.

Two old ladies, who reminded me of my dear, departed grandmother, came in to be provided with new dentures. They filled out and signed the necessary National Assistance Board applications which I posted off to the NAB office in Blyth where inquiries would be made to see if they were entitled to free treatment.

I proceeded with the work since both badly needed new teeth but when the dentures were ready I realised I hadn't heard from the Board. On contacting them again I was told everything was in order and I could proceed and the ladies got their dentures. Weeks passed and when I hadn't received the cheque from the National Assistance I rang them again to be told the old ladies had withdrawn their applications on the day they had received their new teeth. Obviously they knew they weren't entitled to free treatment and, of course, I never saw them again. I was out of pocket because I had to pay among other expenses the technicians who made the dentures.

Those old ladies knew how to work the system and they got their teeth for nothing – a very sad and salutary lesson.

Foreign visitors were entitled to treatment under the NHS and I was once visited by two American ladies who had dentures fitted at a cost of £4 10s each (£4 50p).

They told me in the States one had paid £180 and the other £212 to be fitted with their previous dentures and that if I practised there I would no doubt have a big house, a cabin in the hills, a boat and possibly my own aeroplane! A sobering thought!

My humour was somehow not

Frank in front of the dental surgery.

appreciated by the lady who came in to be fitted with new dentures shortly after one New Year's Eve. She had, she said, drunk too much and vomited her teeth into the toilet and flushed the dentures away.

"Oh dear," I said, "that really was an inconvenience" thinking she would share the joke. The patient solemnly agreed with me! I don't think the dental chair is conducive to humour appreciation.

I realised though I was getting on when I found myself receiving some very odd looks when I asked some patients for their NHS number and saying: "You know, it's on your identity card or old ration book." Some of these patients hadn't been born during the war!

My regulars became friends as well as patients, some having attended as children then adults, then with their own children and in some cases even grandchildren. With only a handful of exceptions they were all lovely people and I knew I'd miss their regular visits when I retired.

That day came on a Friday evening when I left 42 Marine Terrace for the last time and headed for my home in Middleton Street. My wife, Dorothy, said she saw me coming up the street bowed and shoulders slumped and when I arrived told me I should never have retired.

Strangely enough that Sunday night when I thought I was not going to work the next morning, instead of the expected depression I felt curiously elated despite having enjoyed my dental career up to the very last moment. Since then I can honestly say I have thoroughly enjoyed my retirement and the casual meetings and reminiscences with former patients as I walk around Blyth.

A Reporter in Blyth

Jim Harland was born in Beaumont Street, Blyth, on the June 25th, 1935, and was educated at Wright Street Infants School, Princess Louise Road Primary, Crofton Junior School, Princess Louise Road Senior School, Skerry's College, Newcastle and South Shields Marine and Technical College. Before leaving home he lived with his mother and father – who was winding engineman at the Isabella Pit – and siblings – variously at 39 Salisbury Street, 80 Twentieth Avenue, 11 Seventh Avenue and 63 Shelley Crescent. He had a newspaper career which included weekly, bi-weekly, daily and national newspapers and BBC radio and television.

Wellington House, just off Waterloo Road, was where the Northumberland Education Committee careers' officer was situated and it was to there I walked from Princess Louise Road Senior School, where I was head boy, one afternoon in 1950. "And what would you like do when you leave school?" I was asked. "A newspaper reporter," I replied. The man tutted and said: "I'm afraid you have no chance." At the time he was probably right as I had not taken up further education at that time.

Two years later though, not 150 yards from Wellington House, I was earning a living as a junior reporter on the Blyth News – Ashington Post. I have to admit I was rather lucky to enter the fourth estate having spotted a small advertisement in the Journal seeking a junior reporter for the Morpeth Herald. At the time I had been offered a job as a LNER clerk at Newsham Railway Station and with the cockiness of youth I sent off a letter declining the offer at the same time as applying for the reporting job. My extra education after leaving Princess Louise school included becoming a rather speedy shorthand writer and typist – a tremendous advantage in the newspaper game with verbatim notes being taken at courts and councils and so I was offered, and accepted, the job for the princely sum of 35 shillings a week – £1.75 in present day currency.

I shall be ever grateful for the 18 months I spent at Morpeth, travelling daily on my seven shillings and sixpence, twelve journey ticket on the Service 47 and 48 United buses. It gave me a basic grounding in that you never walked past a shop which had posters in the window – posters which on occasions yielded quite decent stories.

My move to the Blyth News, which had its office in Waterloo Road, introduced me to the world of bi-weekly journalism. We published on a Monday and a Thursday which meant working on a Sunday morning. The only remaining sign of that office is the first floor reporters' room above the Shelter charity shop. It is set back and can only been seen from the Market Place. The rest of the building was swallowed up when Northumbria House, which housed the Co-op store, was built.

My switch to the Blyth News brought me back in touch with memories of my early years. Walking down as a five year old from our terraced house in Salisbury Street with outside toilet to Thompson's shop, opposite the Cowpen Quay Post Office, carrying a note for Miss Johnson, the

Alf Robens, former MP for Blyth, visited the town on June 24th, 1964 for the annual inspection of the port as part of his duties as chairman of the National Coal Board. Afterwards he held a press conference when Ray Dunn, the Blyth News photographer captured this shot of me intensely listening to his words wearing, of course, the traditional dirty reporter's mack!

manageress, on which our grocery order was written. The cost of the goods was put in the Tick Book and settled every Friday when my Dad brought home his pay from the pit. It was standard practice by families in our area and you can be assured the book was a fairly thick one! Thompson's stores were widespread in Northumberland and on Tyneside in those days, there was even a larger branch in Blyth in the Arcade Buildings in Waterloo Road now a Pal Joey clothing store.

One of the sons of the business, Bill Thompson was a keen cricketer who played for Blyth for many years as a wicket-keeper/batsman. I got to know him in his later years when he became President of the club.

It is quite remarkable to think that at one time the town of Blyth was supporting twelve journalists. Two covering for the Kemsley newspapers – the Journal, Chronicle and Sunday Sun – and the rest on the Blyth News. Now there is not one reporter based in the town.

We had an editor, Bill Hogg, his brother John who was sub-editor, photographer Jack Nicholson, who later set up his own photographers business in Croft Road, and a chief reporter and five reporters. One of the reporters was Allan Powell who eventually became news editor at Tyne Tees Television and later the Teesside reporter for BBC Look North.

It was Blyth born John Ritson, one of the reporters, who got himself into the black books of the Blyth News management when he damaged the brand new office van used by reporters on their district calls. John forgot to put the hand brake on when parking in Bedlington and the van rolled down Front Street and smashed into the monument in the Market Place causing a fair amount of damage.

One regret I had on joining the Blyth News was that I was too late to go back to Princess Louise Modern School to interview Ted Short. By now he was an MP and starting a political career which took him to deputy leader of the Labour Party and

Blyth Market Place.

several cabinet posts and eventually elevation to the Upper House as Lord Glenamara. He had arrived at the school in 1946 and although extremely active in local politics in Newcastle spent a considerable time trying to improve the school. One innovation was a drama club and I can recall appearing as a policeman in a one act play called *The Bishop's Candlesticks* which was performed on a small stage in the school hall.

In my first book, *True Tales of Blyth*, I tell of how after the school Ted Short managed to gets funds for a complete redecoration of the school of which he was very proud as it had not been refurbished for years.

Pens with nibs were still in use in schools in those days and it was common practise for bored pupils to dip rolled up pieces of paper into the desk ink wells and flip them off the end of wooden rulers on to the ceiling where they stuck and eventually dried out to hang forever. Our class of over thirty was in our room when Ted Short came to investigate after our maths teacher, Mr Castiaux had spotted this vandalism, and one could tell by his face that he was extremely annoyed. He asked for the culprit or culprits to own up. While the two guilty ones were seated in the back of the class they didn't own up. Shorty, as he was known throughout the school, behind his back of course, said he would give us half an hour for the miscreants to confess or he would cane the whole class. To this day I cannot understand why we did not force the two culprits to own up – possibly because they were the class leaders – anyhow we lined up in the corridor before walking up the stairs to his office to get three on each hand from the future Minister for Education.

I can, however, thank Lord Glenamara for aiding me in my journalistic career for he launched a school newspaper. He had already rated one of my poems so highly he had it printed and distributed to every pupil.

The school had an old fashioned printer and trays of type which was in a converted loft space over one of the wash rooms. You got to it by climbing a set of rickety ladders – fortunately Health and Safety was virtually non existent those days – and it was there we regularly produced a four page issue and a school magazine.

A great supporter of Mr. Short at the school was Mr. Bart Peel, his deputy, and a teacher who was highly respected by the pupils. John Jures, who opened the batting for Blyth, was the history master. He had been having a run of low scores and I bet him half a crown I would score more than him when I played for the school on Saturday morning than he would for Blyth first team that afternoon.

I thought the 12 runs I got was more than sufficient because of his poor form but he scored his first fifty of the season! On the Monday morning at school I offered him the cash. It was part of the seven shillings and sixpence I got each week as a paper boy from the Hayward sisters whose newsagents shop in Church Street is now the fruiterers next to where the health shop now stands. He declined to take it but I insisted and eventually he pocketed it as I told him if I had won I certainly would have taken his cash!

As a junior reporter you were quickly thrown into the run of things covering courts at Bedlington and Blyth and councils at Blyth, Seaton Valley and Newbiggin but within 18 months I was back in Morpeth working for Kemsley Newspapers for the Chronicle, Journal and Sunday Sun.

I did not return to the Blyth News until 1958 when the office had moved from Waterloo Road to a building which was situated where the market place entrance to the Mall now stands. The first floor reporters' room was in a much better position as it overlooked the market place and the Police Box. It may be hard to believe now but several constables used to meet almost hourly at the box to report in to the station by telephone.

One of my assignments was the cutting of the first sod at the site for the Blyth B Power Station. It was still possible to drive on to the chain ferry to North Blyth, manned by the skipper Seaman Warnes who lived with his family in Twentieth Avenue, and cut off a detour of several miles via Bedlington Station and East Sleekburn. Ironically, years later, I watched the demolition of the chimneys on that same building.

Another episode I remember clearly was when early one evening in 1959 I heard the maroons, which summon the lifeboat crew to answer an emergency, go off. They could be heard all round the town and further afield. On checking with Tom Fawcus the coxswain of the Blyth lifeboat, *Winston Churchill*, I found they were being called out to help the *Holderness*, a 982 ton collier, which had run aground in rough seas off the East Pier.

She had just left the port when she was caught by a strong south easterly wind and heavy seas and was grounded on rocks less than 50 yards from the East Pier Lighthouse.

Using the chain ferry I walked towards the South Pier where I found a group of

Holderness on rocks.

policemen and onlookers. A breeches buoy had been attached to the collier and before I knew it I was one of a number of onlookers called upon to help haul individual members of the crew over the huge waves on to the pier. The *Winston Churchill* had taken off four of the crew but the remaining nine, including five young Scotsman who had just signed on, were ferried to the pier by the

Holderness in half.

breeches buoy. As expected by locals the *Holderness* was doomed and indeed split in two parts within days of the grounding.

Running the Blyth News office at that time was a golfing cartel – all members of the Blyth Golf Club which was then a 12 hole course to the east of Plessey Road. The editor was Ronnie Cross, the chief reporter Andy Easton, a very much larger figure of life, and Ray Dunn the chief photographer. In addition John Ritson, later to become news editor of the Evening Chronicle in Newcastle, was also a golfing fanatic while the sports editor, Bob Thompson – "Crofter" of Blyth Spartans fame – never, as far as I knew, swung a club. In charge of the office was Ronnie George.

Only John Ritson is still with us, playing golf on the 18-hole golf course built on former Delaval Colliery land in Newsham which runs alongside the former Newsham to Ashington rail line. John is living in retirement in Seaton Sluice.

Several pits, a thriving port trade and a bustling shipyard meant you were never short of stories back in the 50's and 60's. The old adage "People make news" was never truer. Next door to the Blyth News office was the Commercial Inn – the unofficial headquarters of the many ladies of the night who frequented the town chasing the foreign merchant seamen – on whose site Greggs the Bakers now stands – the bakers taking over from the closed Northern Rock office.

Burtons the Tailors, which was next to the Commercial, is still upholding the tradition of dressing the men and boys of the town. In those days it was the Fifty Shilling Tailors and apparently before my time if you bought a suit they threw in free dancing lessons in a studio above the building, later occupied by the Inland Revenue but now by a firm of solicitors.

Blyth boasted a large number of visible business personalities. Harold Blakeborough, who launched the first travel agency in his one roomed sweetie shop just around the corner from the Blyth News office, now the 121 driving school office; Ernie Gallon who ran a record and music shop in Bridge Street where the Dolly Dimples coffee shop now operates; Alex Haxon who had a men's clothing shop in Waterloo Road which is now a bookies; Harry Harper with his fresh fish shop in the Market Place, now a café and ice cream parlour and Tucker Willis and Frank Hardy who had an estate agents in Union Street which is now a sandwich shop

Alan Harper, one of the sons of the Harper family, was wicketkeeper for Blyth cricket team for a few years before leaving the town while Graham Heatley, son of T.G. Heatley who had an estate agents in Bridge Street, also played for Blyth and Northumberland.

Marriage and the need for a bigger pay packet meant a return to the Evening Chronicle and Journal and eventually the post as chief reporter of the Blyth area based in Seaforth Street – opposite the Blyth and Tyne and the Blyth Labour Rooms. I took over an office once run by Johnny Brownlee, a Blyth born journalist, who moved to

Newcastle as the news editor of the Evening Chronicle. Johnny lived in 19 Middleton Street and I can remember as a teenager baby-sitting his son Geoff who later became a senior public relations executive with a large company in the Cleveland area where he also lives with his retired parents on a large country estate.

Newmans bakery and coffee shop in Waterloo Road, next to the newsagents, was a regular haunt for journalists as it was there the insurance agents of the town met every morning. Insurance agents were a great source of tip-offs – two of the

Back row: Jim Harland, Ray Dunn. Middle row: Ronnie Cross, Andy Easton, Alex Moir (South Shields), George Richardson. Front row: John Ritson, Ronnie George.

regulars were Eddie Watson, who was also a fine pianist, and Jimmy Bell, a tenor and independent councillor, who later became secretary of Blyth Operatic Society.

In those days journalists were respected and trusted. We used to do morning calls – not by telephone as they do nowadays – but by walking or driving around various places such as the fire station, police station, the harbourmaster's office. You were known by your first name and indeed at the police station, when you walked into the front office opposite the Star and Garter, the desk sergeant would turn the incidents book towards you so you could see what had happened during the night. Nowadays you are asked to ring the Press Office in the Ponteland headquarters.

Police Superintendant J.D. Patterson, in charge of the Blyth division, was a senior officer who trusted the press. On one occasion he rang me at one o'clock in the morning saying he was off to East Sleekburn to investigate a murder and would I like to come. I had visited his home several times as a guest of his daughter, Jean, who was one of our crowd which went socialising and dancing in our teens.

On the political front I was fortunate from a reporter's point of view to be working in the town during the Labour Party turmoil brought about by Eddie Milne taking over as MP from Alf Robens, who went on to be chairman of the National Coal Board. Eddie, a former Co-op clerk and union leader in Edinburgh, upset a number of the party officials and members and as a result there was a constant flow of interesting news stories, two of which, written by me were referred to the Press Complaints Council by the MP – and were rejected out of hand.

One of the more poignant assignments I had occurred on November 2nd, 1964, with the closure of the Blyth railway line which took you to Newcastle or Ashington, brought about by the Beeching plan which decimated the railway system in Britain. It had been decided to run the last train at midnight and so, along with scores of other passengers, I boarded the train at Blyth. It took us through Newsham station which was also being closed, passed Bebside station which had been shut since 1956 and on into Ashington then made the return journey.

That was one of the sad memories I took away when my reporting stint in Blyth came to an end in 1965 after I accepted an invitation to join the Sunday Mirror in Manchester.

War and the Boys' Club

Jack Allen BEM was born in Beaumont Street on September 15th, 1923, the only child of a colliery fitter and worked in Blyth Shipyard, Bates Colliery, on board coal colliers out of the river Blyth until taking up youth work as the full time leader of Blyth Town Boys' Club and as a grown man he also embarked on a most unusual hobby.

Morpeth Road Infants School, hardly a stones throw away from our terraced house, was where I began my education. It followed I would go on to the Morpeth Road Junior school and eventually the Princess Louise Road Senior School which was a little longer walk and that was where I stayed until I was 14.

Two years earlier tragedy had struck the family when my Dad was killed when a wall fell on him while working at Cowpen Colliery which was in the area near where the Lidl store now stands – in fact the old colliery offices are now an old people's home. With Dad dying we had eventually to move out of the colliery house. My mother fought a long battle for compensation and eventually won enough to get us our own home – a bungalow costing £450 at 410 Plessey Road just alongside the old Cosimini's fish shop near the first rail crossing.

Even though we now lived a fair distance from the town centre I continued my memberhip of the Blyth Town Boys' Club which was run by Bill Ogilvy, a Scotsman. It was affiliated to the National Association of Boys' Clubs, and had begun life in the upstairs rooms of the Arcade Buildings near the Market Place – later to become an Chinese restaurant then the Clock Cafe – but eventually moved to the Irish Club in Wright Street. The club is no longer there as it was demolished many years ago to make way for houses and flats. Fortunately the more suitable Wright Street Infants School closed in 1940 and the club was able to move.

Jack Allen.

I started work with Blyth Council as an apprentice joiner and was there for two years when war broke out. I wanted to do something to help so without my mother's knowledge went to the recruiting office in Blyth. I signed on for the Merchant Navy but it came as a surprise when they told me I would be sailing that night and that I had to go and pack a bag.

I went home and broke the news to my mother by saying I needed to pack a bag and telling her what was up. She took my decision very calmly and I cannot recall her saying anything. Off I went to the dockside and joined the collier the SS *Slemish*. It was on that maiden trip that I had my first encounter with the German Luftwaffe which was to leave me temporarily deaf.

We were off Flamborough Head when the alarm sounded. Being a newcomer I hadn't be given an alarm position and I found myself standing underneath the barrel of our twelve pounder gun. An able seamen handed me a tin hat and a Lewis machine gun. I'd never seen one before never mind fire it. But fire it I did when someone shouted: "There it is." It was pitch black and I couldn't see a thing but I fired the gun. It was quite exhillarating and I continued firing into the dark. It was only later when a Royal Navy frigate appeared we learned I had strafed the rigging of another collier. Anyhow while I was firing the twelve pounder went off. Now no-one told me not to stand underneath such a gun or that it made such a huge bang. As a result I couldn't hear a thing for hours much to the amusement of the crew.

My stint on the colliers, and I served on several of them, led to trips, before the Germans invaded, across to France but mainly we carried coal around the British coast until I was medically discharged in 1945 having damaged my right knee. I didn't fancy a return to the council so I joined the shipyard. The money wasn't too good so I went to Bates Colliery where the money was better but the job as a bumper looking after the roadways and suspect tunnel roofs was one of the worst in the pit.

I had resumed my membership of the Boys' Club. Before the war I had been involved in instructing and teaching model making and when Bill Ogilvy decided to retire I applied and got the leader's job. I didn't realise at that time it was to last 37 years.

I soon found out there wasn't an awful lot of money around in those days and it was a matter of begging and borrowing to keep the club running. The Northumberland County Youth Service gave us an annual grant but this was subject to an inspection by the County Youth Organiser, Miss Valerie Tully, who lived in Bedlington. Fortunately the county money, although not an awful lot, kept coming and I was able to introduce boxing, cricket and woodwork into the curriculum for the 100 or so regulars who came to the club. Tropical fish were also put on the agenda and our large tank was a popular attraction.

There were some characters among the membership some good, some bad. On one occasion the café section was broken into during the night and a large box of liquorice sticks was stolen. The culprit though was quite easy to find as the box was open and he didn't realise he was dropping a trail of sticks right up to his home, which was quite close to the club. Actually he wouldn't have been difficult to trace as he was the only member who had

A young Jack Allen making a model boat.

a permanent craving for licorice. Subsequent events led to me clashing with David Baron the chairman of the Blyth magistrates.

The lad was due to appear in court and as his father couldn't afford to lose a day's pay his mother asked me to go with the boy to the Juvenile Court which was held in a small court room at Blyth Police Station. The chairman on this day was David Baron, who had a chemist's shop in the town and was a former Mayor. Although he knew me, we were on Christian name terms, he asked me if I was a relative and when I said I wasn't he ordered me out.

I was rather shocked and annoyed and tackled him that night at his regular drinking haunt, the Royal Tavern. I told him I thought his action had been wrong and while accepting there were privacy rules in a juvenile court, with access limited to family members, I had been there to speak on behalf of the boy. I also told him I knew that part of the sentence he gave had been to order the boy to attend the Boys' Club three nights a week. I said I should have been in court and asked if I was agreeable to the arrangement. Give him his due David apologised and we remained friends up to his death.

But there was one incident which made me proud. A member of the club was a lad called Hewson Taylor who, in later life, was to sing leading roles in the local operatic society. I was refereeing an indoor soccer match in the club when I noticed a police constable standing at the top of the stairs.

I went over to him, took him downstairs, and asked if I could help. He said he needed to speak to a Hewson Taylor. I said he was playing football and I would get him. I left the two of them in my office.

At the end of the night I beckoned Hewson to the office and told him if he was in any kind of trouble I was there to help. He looked surprised and said: "No, it's nothing like that. A couple of weeks ago I found a ten bob note in the Market Place and took it to the police station. The officer had come to give it back to me as it had not been claimed."

When I took over the Boys' Club we had a membership of over 70 and during my time there it reached a peak of over 200 with queues forming in the street at night until it opened.

On one occasion the club committee received a letter on behalf of a professional singer who wanted to put on a concert in the town to raise funds for the National Association of Boys' Clubs. Now the committee was made up of well meaning adults who voluntarily gave up their time to help run the club. I was asked: "Who is this Frankie Vaughan?"

Frankie subsequently became president of the National Association of Boys' Clubs, having been a club member in the south himself, and the concert in the Newlands School Hall, now the site of the Bede Academy, was arranged.

At that time one of my hobbies was travelling around the area with a group entertaining the old folk and any organisation that needed entertainment. Our group, the Gimmicracks, was composed of me, Alan Hetherington, who was a football referee, and Bob Millican, the brother of Alan who found fame and record success in the Millican and Nesbitt duo.

We sang close harmony, solos and added in a bit of comedy. Anyhow we were part of the concert in Newlands along with Frankie Riley, Blyth's singing cobbler, and Stan Beckwith the one armed trumpet player and singer, also a local lad.

It was such a success that Frankie Vaughan invited us all to appear with him at another concert in aid of the NABC in Sunderland.

Frankie paid a couple of visits to Blyth and just a few years ago I was looking forward to meeting him again at the Wallaw where he was due to give a show. Unfortunately he took ill and while the concert was postponed he never recovered and died.

Frankie Vaughan on the piano at a NABC talent contest.

Meeting Frankie was a highlight but the other two treasured memories are of being awarded the British Empire Medal for my services to the NABC and getting the Freedom of the Borough of Blyth.

People often asked me what I did away from the Boys' Club. Well, I'm a magpie, I collect things. I have coin collections and stamp collections but my pride and joy is my collection of model cars. It was a hobby I took up as I approached middle age. I have over 400 of them and have them displayed in cabinets, which I made, in two of the rooms in my house. Actually the manufacturers of the cars contact me with news of their latest models to give me first choice.

Yes, collecting things is my hobby.

One of my great joys now though is to walk around the town and recognize businessmen and other former members of the club who have made a success of their lives. It brings on a feeling of well being in that I believe I have contributed, in some small way, to help them to that success.

Jack Allen with his model cars.

The Commando and Blyth Council

Alf Barker was born in Manchester on February 26th, 1915, but spent the major part of his life contributing to the administrative side of Blyth as the deputy town clerk of the

Borough Council and Borough Secretary following the amalgamation with Seaton Valley Urban Council. He now lives alone in Seaton Sluice having survived two wives. Alf served in the Commandoes during the Second World War, was evacuated from Dunkirk in a small boat but returned to take part in the D-Day landings. Asked if he ever killed a man he says: "Not that I was aware of. I fired my gun though."

Alf Barker today.

The first sight of Blyth in 1959, other than from the train from Newsham, was a dilapidated wooden tobacco kiosk standing in front of the station bearing a Finlays sign. It was a dull, dingy day and had been raining. As I stood there I asked myself what on earth I had done applying for the job of Deputy Town Clerk to Blyth Borough Council.

I had been booked in to the Star and Garter Hotel and made my way there following directions from a local. And it was there I met the famous Mrs Donachie, rich in Scottish accent, and a stickler for the licensing hours. She kept a well run pub and hotel even though it was situated close to the dockside area which also did not paint in my eyes an attractive picture of the town.

Alf Barker at his desk in 1969.

There were six in for the job and the interviews took place the next day. It was a rather large interview panel made up of councillors and officials and it was then I set my eyes on Edwin Carter, the town clerk, a man who I was later to find out was straight as a die, an excellent boss and who brooked no interference, councillors or not. I also met for the first time Alderman Fred Smith and Councillor Gilbert Barker, two of the council stalwarts who were not the best of friends and Councillor Alex Rutherford.

After the interviews we sat in an anteroom for what seemed an age. I discovered later why. Eventually I was invited in and offered the job. I accepted but knew in my heart I would be turning it down.

Another of the applicants was staying at the Blyth and Tyne and that night I told him as he had been runner up to prepare himself to be offered the job as I intended writing a letter turning it down.

I never did write that letter because of a bus ride I took the next day while waiting to catch my train from Blyth to Newcastle. The bus took me along the Links and I was astonished at the openness of the area, the beach and the many fields. What a difference. The contrast was amazing and I realised I had been misled by my first sight of the area.

By now I was married with a son and daughter and while Ada, my wife, who worked in the Stockport magistrates clerks department, was a bit apprehensive, we moved to the town having been allocated a council house at 154 Newsham Road. It had been lived in by an old lady and was badly neglected. The cooker was caked in dirt and the whole place needed cleaning from top to bottom. To say Ada was a bit shocked was an understatement as indeed I was. I was fortunate in that one of the cleaners at the council offices heard of the problem and brought the house up to scratch in her own time for which she was handsomely rewarded.

Fortunately six months later Charlie Gurney, the housing officer, who later became a firm friend, was able to get us a better house in St Ronan's Drive, Seaton Sluice. It was a brilliant move as Ada and I fell in love with the village and that is where we settled when we bought our bungalow and where I still live today.

Having gained local government experience in Stockport after becoming a chartered secretary while working for the Manchester Co-operative Society through the Co-op educational scheme, I quickly settled in thanks the help of new friends including the local bookie, Percy Hardy.

People often asked me if I understood the Geordie lingo when I arrived. Actually I had no trouble with it in Blyth but one day Percy offered to show me the area by taking me on his rounds collecting bets in local pubs and social clubs.

It was when we got to Bomarsund Social Club that I thought I could have been in China. I just could not understand a word they were saying and Percy, amid laughter, had to translate.

I soon learned what high regard my boss, Edwin Carter, was held as his advice to all and sundry was never ignored – and that included the powerful figures on the council.

The arrival of Eddie Milne as MP following the departure of Alf Robens for the chairmanship of the National Coal Board began quietly but there were mutterings when he started attending the monthly council meetings, sitting in the public gallery.

He soon began interfering in departments

Eddie Milne, the Blyth MP, was asked to take up the case of dangerous, redundant air raid shelters in the yard of the Cowpen Catholic School. Accompanied by Father Gibbons and some of the children he carried out an inspection of the shelters on September 18th, 1969. The shelters were demolished some time later.

of the council. When he did it in mine, I cannot actually remember what it was about, I decided to confront him at the end of a council meeting. In front of the Mayor, I took the MP to task for what I regarded as something outside his remit. I was fully backed by the Mayor and other councillors and the interference ceased.

The major event to happen during my tenure was when the government in 1974 introduced a bill to amalgamate councils as a cost cutting measure. It meant Blyth Borough was amalgamated with Seaton Valley Urban Council and included part of Whitley Bay Borough Council. At the same time the urban councils of Ashington and Newbiggin were formed into Wansbeck.

As far as we were concerned there was the problem of having two town clerks, Edwin for Blyth and Peter Ferry for Seaton Valley. Edwin solved that problem by retiring and Peter took the top job while I was designated Borough Secretary.

While, naturally, Peter leant a little towards Seaton Valley – the Blyth councillors were told in no uncertain terms to keep their hands off Cramlington – the switchover was smooth and although initially there was a surfeit of councillors until the wards were re-aligned it was, in the main, successful.

Peter Ferry.

The closure of Bates Pit, which was the last colliery in the town, in 1985 had a major effect on the running of the council. With no contributions from the pit the Cowpen and Crofton Welfare in Renwick Road was financially strapped and the council, finding the amalgamation had brought an increased pressure for more room, purchased the building. The imposing Council and Mayor's chambers in the Freehold Street building continued until the complete handover took place which allowed a major change in the town – the Keel Row Shopping Mall – to come into being.

Although the council supported a public demand that the Theatre Royal be saved there was no action the council could take as compulsory purchase orders had not been sought. The old council building, the Theatre Royal, the Alexandra Billiard Hall and the T. & B. Garage along with the Methodist Church made way for the Shopping Mall and adjoining car park.

As an official of the council for 27 years I witnessed the fascinating changes which have taken place in the borough – some good, some bad. The down side was the closure of the shipyard and the pits but on the other hand the town centre, which almost put me off coming, and other areas have undergone welcome transformations. To sum up "Coming to Blyth was the best move I ever made."

Edwin Carter, the town clerk of Blyth, receives from the mayor, Alderman James W. Kennedy, a silver salver presented to Blyth Borough Council by Blyth TA. The ceremony took place in the Council Chamber in Seaforth Street on November 9th, 1961.

The Wonder of Woolies

The closure of Woolworth's store in January, 2009, brought to an end more than seventy years of its prominent position in Blyth Market Place. Throughout the years it had on occasions had a staff of over fifty but the gradual introduction of new sales methods led to a drastic reduction in employees. It opened, as did all other branches in Britain as a 3d and 6d store, that's just over one pence and two pence in today's money where goods cost just that, but the sign disappeared shortly after the Second World War.

Two former employees of F.W. Woolworth, both 86, tell of their experiences working for the American-owned company – Doreen Younger who lives in Plessey Road, and Joan Waddle who lives in Princess Louise Road.

Doreen Younger Memories

It was in 1956 when I joined initially as an assistant on the biscuits and cakes section where we spent a lot of time slicing the huge cakes which were sold by the pound. We had angel cakes, fruit cakes and rice cakes and at the end of the day we had to scrape the cake crumbs off the floor because we had been so busy there had not been time during the day.

Anyone on the biscuits and cakes counter had to wear white overalls which were so starched you felt like a robot for a while. My move to groceries meant a change of uniform this time to maroon red – they were horrible but they weren't so stiff.

The one advantage of the move was I could buy my tea for home from Bob Robinson who was a rep for Walter Willson's in Blyth who regularly called at our counter. Whereas nowadays buying is done on a centralised system representatives were allowed to call at our counter where we could order goods not only for the store but also for ourselves.

Doreen Younger.

Woolworth's was in an old building which still had a coke-fired boiler and large heating pipes. One of these pipes ran along the back of our counter and because there was a tremendous demand for jellies – orange, lemon, blackcurrant, raspberry and strawberry we were forever having to go upstairs to the stock room for supplies.

I decided, however, to get large boxes of the different types put behind the counter near the pipes, which were not on at the time. Someone, however, decided it was cold and turned the central heating on and we soon found ourselves sloshing around melted jellies in double quick time. That incident had to be reported, ironically enough, in the book used for recording losses of goods. It was known officially as the Shrinkage Book! The one thing I felt strange about was that all the staff, irrespective of whether they were married or not, were called by their maiden names prefixed by Miss. No-one could tell us why this was so – you certainly weren't asked at your interview if you were married or single.

Another job you weren't told about at the start was that you were expected to take your turn at polishing the brasses each morning on the front doors and to oil the wooden floor of the store on a Saturday night.

This wasn't a bone of contention but one that certainly was among the staff came about because all the industries in the town, the shipbuilding, shipbreaking and mines, all took the last week in July and the first week in August as their annual holidays. As it also coincided with arrival of hundreds of Scots on their Wakes Week it made it one of the busiest shopping periods and meant only about four of the staff could take holidays with their husbands. It was the unwritten rule in the shop that the longest serving got the two weeks and we were not very happy – the same thing happened at Christmas.

Woolworth's in Blyth was an extremely cold building particularly early in the day when we were soon frozen as there was no timed heating with it being coke-fired. Had we had a union we no doubt would have walked out on occasions. Instead we just accepted things and indeed helped the stockroom staff, all women, stoke the boilers when the temperatures dropped – one of many jobs women on the staff did which they would not dream of doing now or indeed would not be allowed to – health and safety and all that stuff.

It was while I was on the grocery section that I had my accident. I was carrying a large sack of sugar when I badly hurt my back. The injury was so severe I ended up in plaster for ten weeks. Mind you the bosses were sympathetic and I was offered a compensation choice – a pension or a lump sum. I chose the cash – £360, a very welcome sum in those days. When I eventually returned to work I was appointed supervisor on the cosmetics counter where we spent our time selling the popular Snowfire Cream and Ponds Cold Cream.

Social occasions were popular with employees of F.W. Woolworth as can be seen by the large number at this dinner in the Blyth Co-operative café in Waterloo Road.

Electrical Fitments

One of the walls in the shop stocked oilcloth which was in general use then not only to cover floors but also to use in cupboards, shelves and ledges. Another household product we sold was curtain wire which we would cut to the appropriate length for the customer and put the hooks on either end. A lady came in and was asked what size she wanted cutting. She replied "I don't know – it's for a council house window."

It was also the time when electrical fitments came without plugs and many a customer would ask us to fit the plugs to lamps they had bought which we did. It all stopped when all the staff got a memo from the management saying the practice had to cease. We were given no reason but assumed it was because someone, somewhere, had wrongly wired up a plug and caused some kind of accident.

In the main everyone got on well with each other at Woolworth's until a new manager was appointed who turned out to be a right bad one. He was making things very uncomfortable for us. It reached such a state that a friend, Nancy Martin, me and another girl were so unhappy at his attitude that we left and went to work in the Ronson Hair Dryer factory which had just opened in Cramlington.

It was the most boring work on a production line doing the same thing time after time, day after day. After a couple of months Agnes Biggs, the senior supervisor at Woolworth's, contacted us and said the manager had been sacked and we could have our jobs back. And so I stayed until I had to retire in 1985 on reaching the age of 60.

On rare occasions photographs of the entire Woolworth's staff were taken. The late Nancy Martin, who worked many years for the company, uncovered one taken in the 1950's outside the store in the Market Place, and passed it on to the author. Nancy is seated third from the right in the second row.

Joan Waddle's Memories

Like Doreen I too worked initially on the cake and biscuits counter and the thing I remember most is the fixation the management had about wastage. The boss was forever coming behind our counter to check and to reprimand us if we had too many broken biscuits. It was impossible not to have any as quite a few of the boxes they arrived in had already been damaged. All the broken ones were put in a box behind the counter and eventually sold off cheaply in bags – they were very popular with the youngsters.

Also as our large cakes had to be cut to order by weight we tried our best not to be left with small pieces which couldn't be sold – it was quite a challenge.

Eventually I was transferred to the toy counter and it was a job I thoroughly enjoyed although I didn't get away from the attention of the boss. I had a large glass funnel on the counter which was filled with inflated balloons on the end of a stick – a very popular seller – and I had to blow the balloons up. He would come and say, in a rich Scot's voice: "I think we should keep that funnel filled don't you think Miss Tweedy?" That meant a few minutes hard work with the inflator.

Joan Waddle and her late husband, Norman, pictured in 1962 at the Roxy Ballroom where Norman was a saxophonist and violinist in the orchestra.

As Doreen explained it was the custom to call all members of the staff by their maiden names and it proved rather embarrassing on one occasion when I was upstairs in the stockroom. A member of staff shouted up the stairs in front of customers: "Your son's here Miss Tweedy."

As we neared Christmas time customers would bring their children in and if the youngster got their eye on a toy they fancied they would ask if Santa was going to bring it for

Retirements of Woolworth's staff and other presentations were usually held in the Star and Garter Hotel, regarded as the premier hotel in Blyth, supervised by the ultra efficient manageress, Mrs Donachie.

them. A glance at the mother would tell whether they could afford it or not and you gave your response accordingly. It was after an incident like this I suggested to the management that we started a Christmas Club which would allow parents to pay in money so the cost of the toy was eventually covered. They paid the money direct to the accounts department and the scheme worked very successfully because in those days there was not a lot of money around in Blyth.

The running of Woolworth's was very regimented. Every item on your counter had to be written down and we all had leather pouches into which we put our takings, all balanced up, which were collected nightly by a member of the Accounts Department. She had a much bigger leather satchel into which all the satchels were put and I felt sorry for her having to carry such a weight of all the money particularly near the end of her round.

New Year's Eve though could be a nightmare with the annual stocktaking. When we finished itemising all the toys and making out our hand-written list we had to go to the hardware section and help them out. It was one heck of a task counting all the individual nails and screws.

The counter staff on New Year's Eve, however, were more fortunate than the girls in Accounts. I was told that on one occasion they were still in the store at six o'clock in the morning and that one of the supervisors had earlier gone to a chemists to get pills that would allow them to stay awake during the stocktaking. I still managed to see the New Year in at home or at a party. Happy days!

Dress discipline at Woolworths was loosened in the 1970's as can be seen by this staff photograph taken outside the store. Gone were the maroon red counter staff uniforms and the white starched ones – a must if you worked in the bakery and biscuits section.

The Golfing Centenarian

Edith Mitcheson is 100 and during fine weather can be seen on the greens of Blyth Golf Club pitching and putting with two of her friends. She was born at 32 Claremont Terrace, Blyth, on May 10th, 1910, to Arthur, a train driver, and Kate Thompson. Now in a comfortable sheltered accommodation flat in New Hartley Court, in the village of the same name, she tells in her own words of different aspects of her life involving teaching, marriage to Harry Mitcheson, later to become general manager of Blyth Dry Docks and Shipbuilding company and sport – her all consuming hobby – particularly golf.

Throughout this time Edith heavily indulged in sport – netball and hockey at school and tennis in the evenings. Initially she and her friends played tennis on the courts in Ridley Park but in their teens they joined Blyth Cricket and Tennis Club in Plessey Road. It was there she won several championships and proved herself to be one of the best women players in the club.

In 1936 she won the mixed doubles club championship with Barnes Hodgson. He was so thrilled at winning, and because no permanent trophies were presented, he had two tiny inscribed silver cups made at his own expense and gave one to Edith. It still has pride of place on the window sill of her flat in New Hartley.

"He was really delighted to have won as we were what you would call rank outsiders and I was just as thrilled to get a memento of the occasion," Edith says. One of her close friends nowadays is Joyce her tennis partner's daughter. Edith was captain of the ladies team twice and also held the post of Lady President. These are her memories taken from a family book she prepared for her two grandchildren, Luke and Rebecca, in 1991.

Edith Mitcheson.

The Day War Broke Out

When I was four I visited my paternal grandparents with my parents and my sister Mary who was six and a half years older than me. They lived in a village called Meadowfield, about four miles from the city of Durham. Their home consisted of the house, combined with a newsagent's shop, combined with a large workshop where coffins were made. At the back was a stable in which a horse was housed and next to it a large shed in which there was a carriage. There were no cars in those days.

The first morning after we arrived by train I was in the shop when I heard the sound of galloping horses. Everyone rushed to the front door to see soldiers on horseback galloping from Brancepeth to Durham City. The word went round "War has broken out". I ran to the back of the shop and covered my eyes. I was afraid.

That was the beginning of the First World War which lasted from 1914 to 1918. When I arrived back home that day I flew upstairs, threw myself on the bed, and wept bitterly. A wonderful portion of my life had ended and I was so sad.

Later I saw Zepplins in the sky which seemed to hover over our homes in Blyth. It was incredible, nobody had seen the like. We were all afraid.

School Days

When I was five I went to St Wilfrid's Catholic Infants School and two years later I moved to the Catholic Junior School where I remained until I was eleven. Discipline was strict and we were all terrified of the head teacher, Miss Comer. Believe me, we did as we were told.

My best friends were Anna Flynn and Mary Keenan. Anna and I lived in the same street, Mary just around the corner opposite an empty shed. This meant that we could use the pavement in front of the shed to bat balls up against the walls without disturbing anyone. Not only that but at the back was a field and we used these amenities to the utmost. We whipped tops, we skipped endlessly, we played marbles, we chased and jumped ditches, we learned to handle tennis racquets and all with great enjoyment. If there were any quarrels I don't remember them.

This came to an end when I was eleven. Anna Flynn and I passed the entrance exam to the Secondary School, Mary stayed on at St Wilfrid's and our lives changed. Blyth Secondary School, later the Grammar, was an all girls' school and I attended it from 1922 to 1928. It was non-Catholic and I can only remember about two other Catholics all the time I was there.

During the morning prayers assembly we went to a classroom and chatted and during the weekly religious lesson we sat at the side to read. It reminded me now of Ireland. Thank God for the Churches Together movement which now exists in the town and which priests like Father Lennon have done so much to foster.

My sister Mary had just left the Secondary school to go to college but she was clever and always first or second in the class so when I started I had no identity. I was always Mary Thompson's sister. It wasn't until I was in the third form that I became Edith and on the games field "Teedie T". I had begun to show my games prowess and at the end of that year I was voted in as head of Earsdon House. We had four houses and the captains chose the teams to play against each other.

In the summer we played tennis and cricket and in the winter netball and hockey. I was in my element. In my fifth year I became the school games' captain and in my sixth year I also became Head Prefect. When I left school I was presented with the most prestigious prize of all given to the student who had done most for the school – the 1914-18 War Memorial Prize. I also got two books – *The Plays of Burns* and *The Forsythe Saga*.

In lessons at school I varied from sixth to twelfth out of thirty and left with six O levels and three A levels. I had a good report and was well commended by the head, Miss Murdoch, so I hoped to be able to get into college without difficulty. This proved to be the case.

The Ladies' Section of Blyth Golf Club in 1971. Back row: Grace Kirk, Queenie Thompson, Margaret Beadlen, Ivy Barlow, Elsie Law, Kathy Jackson, Beryl White, Joan Dunn, Margery Mitcheson, Alice Gilbertson. Middle row: Olive Ritson, Enid Gibson, Alice Cooper, Lydia Kinnear, Mary Smith, Doris Hay, Margaret Ferrell, Anne Purcell, Nellie Baker, Jenny Tweedy. Front row: Mildred Eadington, Betty Kirkland, Edith Mitcheson (capt), Liz Foster, Norma Gray, Mary Purcell.

Endsleigh Training College

I had never been away from home in my life and on September 7th, 1928, I travelled by train to Hull and by tram from the station to Beverley where the college was situated. I was dressed all in brown as were all the other students. Fortunately it was a colour that suited me as my hair was very dark, as were my eyes. Brown coat, brown shoes and stockings, brown blazer, everything brown.

I hadn't travelled much but I had always been a free spirit. This college was controlled by nuns. Reverend Mother was Principal and, believe me, she was a tartar. She ran a tight ship and for the first few weeks I didn't think I would be able to stand it, I was so homesick.

I had a nice room overlooking a big field and a settee that pulled into a bed. There was also a desk, a bookcase and a chair so I couldn't grumble. There was a bathroom and toilets at each end of the corridor.

Each morning we were awakened by a loud knock on the door at 6.10 a.m. and the nun's voice cried: "Arise, and bless the Lord." We then had to jump out of bed, open the door, leave it ajar so that it could be seen what we were doing and answer "Thanks be to God." We then washed and dressed and assembled down a set of stairs in the middle corridor in the place we had been given.

I must say we were well fed, we all put weight on, perhaps it was the food, perhaps it was because of the regular life we led. At any rate I settled down although I can never claim to have been really happy and I longed for the Christmas holidays.

Eventually my two years at Endsleigh passed. I sat my final exams and returned home a fully trained teacher to find a job. I was lucky, Princess Louise Road Senior School for Girls needed a games teacher and I was just the ticket. I applied, went for an interview and got the job and started after the summer holidays in 1930.

Edith.

I loved my job. We had a good headmistress and staff and as the discipline was excellent, even though we had classes of up to 42. When I arrived there was only one netball for the whole of the school. I organised a raffle and with the proceeds bought two netballs for each class in the school – twelve classes, twenty four netballs. I had the forms painted on each ball, placed them in a cupboard, easy of access, so that they could use them at playtime and lunchtime.

We had netball practise at least three times a week after school and in the end we had a wonderful school netball team winning the Northumberland and Durham Netball Trophy, a Silver Pegasus, three years running and being allowed to keep it. I believe it is still in Blyth somewhere.

Harry Mitcheson.

The Romance

I met Harry Mitcheson, whom I was eventually going to marry, at the Blyth tennis club. He was a good player and what I liked most was his sense of humour. He could always make me laugh and we fell in love almost at first sight. Wherever I was he turned up and we became great companions. He sought me out each night and gradually we became a pair.

Harry did not have to go into the armed services since he was a naval architect at Blyth shipyard and he was of much more use there than he would have been anywhere else. He designed several warships and I attended the launches of many of them. There is something very exciting and emotional about seeing a ship enter the water for the first time to the cheers of the workers. Later, we would have dinner at the Gosforth Park Hotel or the Station Hotel in Newcastle where we listened to the various speakers.

I had a very busy life. During the day I taught the girls, aged 11 to 14, and at night I was a voluntary ambulance driver. When the siren went I had to make my way down to the Wallaw Cinema garage on a bike and pick up an ambulance which was filled with fire fighters and first aiders, both men and women. We all wore tin hats and dark trousers and coats which were provided for us. They sat in the back on two long benches and often their tin hats bumped causing lots of laughter. There were no lights, just two little ones to guide the ambulance. It was like Dad's Army. Fortunately I was very familiar with the route and drove to Bebside School where I parked and we all waited in the school either for a bomb or for the "all clear" when I had to take them back to Blyth. We were extremely lucky as we only had two bomb raids even though Blyth had a shipyard and was a submarine base. I also slept every Wednesday night, along with Margaret Bligh, another teacher, in the staff room at the Bebside school where we acted as fire watchers. Then it was back to our school at nine o'clock the next morning. No wonder we were tired.

At the end of the street I lived in was a field and when the siren went the RAF used to raise barrage balloons to prevent the German pilots from flying too low. One night as I was cycling down to Blyth all the balloons were in flames. I could easily have been shot but it wasn't to be.

In 1942 Harry and I were married at St Wilfrid's Church in Blyth. Anna Flynn was my bridesmaid and Jack Fairbairn was Harry's best man. The reception was held in the Star and Garter Hotel near the quayside. We went on honeymoon to Rothbury and stayed at the Station Hotel for a week and then we spent a week at our caravan which was in Plessey Woods on the banks of the river Blyth. Remember it was wartime and there was very little petrol. Still we managed to have a great time. We used the caravan constantly during the war cycling there and back to Blyth.

Edith and Harry.

I left teaching when our only child, David, was born in 1948. My mother had two girls, my sister had two girls and I knew nothing about boys. I had to learn. The nurse drummed into me that breast feeding was the best and he should never ever have a bottle. I thought he was going to be breast fed forever but at seven months he had his first bottle. He also never had a dummy as I was told that letting a child suck a dummy gave them protruding teeth. When I see all the contented babies today sucking their dummies I think "Poor little boy". Those nurses duped me!

When David was two Harry and I decided it was time we had our own house as we were living with my parents and we had one built on Broadway, number 54, facing a field and with a nice back garden.

When David was five years old I returned to teaching as a supply teacher standing in for absent staff and one of my assignments was to Newlands Secondary School, a new school built to accommodate 1,000 pupils in mixed classes aged 11 to 15. I wondered how I would get on as I had only ever taught girls but I found boys were easier than the girls – less devious. Anyhow the headmaster, Mr Davies, must have been satisfied because he said there was a job coming up to teach English and he asked me to apply for it. I did so and stayed there for the rest of my working life until 1970, thirty-five years of teaching classes of up to 42 pupils. On my retirement Mr Davies presented me with a crystal decanter and six crystal glasses.

The school was so popular lots of Blyth parents wanted their children to attend Newlands because if they were bright enough they could stay on until they were sixteen and take 'O' levels and so we were always bursting at the seams.

Right: The miniature cup Edith won in 1936 in the Blyth Cricket and Tennis Club mixed doubles competition takes pride of place on the window ledge at her home in New Hartley. Her doubles partner, Barnes Hodgson, was so delighted at winning the competition that he had two silver miniature cups made and gave one to Edith.

Ever-green Edith's still a Tiger at 93

Edith hit the headlines in 2003 when she won the Blyth Past Ladies Captains' trophy at the age of 93.

Harry and Blyth Shipyard

Harry was doing very well in his profession. He was made assistant manager and then manager of Blyth Shipyard which had a work force of 1,000 men of all trades. The yard had been bought by the Moller Brothers, Eric and Budgie, who also had a shipyard in Hong Kong. It was a very stressful time since, after the war, work was difficult to get and the unions were very strong. Whenever it was time for a launch there was always the threat of a strike unless the workers were promised a rise in wages.

Eric Moller had a mansion in Bromley, Surrey, to which Harry, David and I were invited each year for a fortnight's holiday to stay with him and his wife. We found the butler's house was bigger than the one we had moved into in Horton Road from Broadway in 1962. The butler was in charge of all the staff and we were given a beautiful en suite bedroom.

The gates of Blyth shipyard were shut for the last time when two men walked through them. Bill Danskin, who worked in the accounts department, had been appointed acting general manager by the receiver when the company went bankrupt 19 months earlier, and Tom Stephenson who stayed on to dismantle the electrical equipment, some of which he had helped to instal.

In the summer of 1964, overnight, the shipyard went into liquidation. No-one had the least idea, not even Harry. It appeared a political move, the government was getting rid of the shipyards as the war was over and so was the need for them. I'm sure the Moller brothers would do alright from the liquidation. Harry had worked there for 50 years – no golden handshake, no pension. The workers were the same, sacked overnight. Any questions had to be directed to Hong Kong – a very far away place.

Harry wasn't out of work for long having been offered a job by Michael Gregson whose company built and repaired ships. I had the honour of launching one, the *Princess Anne*. Gregsons had moved from North Shields to the new Bebside Industrial Estate in Blyth but unfortunately there was a great lack of work and after ten or twelve years Michael retired and sold the site to Fergusons Transport where they are still based.

Harry then went into business on his own on an industrial site in Plessey Road and he was there until he died quite suddenly at home.

Note: On May 10th, 2010, Edith celebrated her 100th birthday. A huge party was held for her at Blyth Golf Club where she planned to continue showing her putting and pitching skills in fine weather.

Football, Kazoos and Buses

Alan Davison was born on May 28th, 1936, at 39 High Street, Blyth, to Jeremiah, a Cambois miner, and Jean. He was educated at Crofton Infants and Junior schools and then Princess Louise Senior School. On leaving school he spent a year in Wooley Sanatorium with tuberculosis. Alan's contribution to Blyth has been as a football and juvenile jazz band organiser. He has been driving coaches and buses for 49 years and in 2000 was named Blyth's Citizen of the Year.

My involvement in football and the juvenile jazz band scene came about literally by chance when I joined the United bus company in Blyth. I was discharged from the Wooley Sanatorium at the age of 16 and started my first job in Cramlington making coiled springs. That lasted about a year when I began lorry driving with, at varying times, several firms including Redheads Sweets in Blyth and Welch's Sweets in North Shields. But it was on joining the United bus company in 1959 that my life was changed forever.

A Scotsman named George Burney was the organiser in chief at United and was planning a party for the children of employees of the company when he was recalled to Scotland on a family matter and asked me to take over. As he didn't return to Blyth I found I had taken over his mantle as organiser. This also brought me into contact with football as the company had an inter-depot competition.

Alan Davison.

From that beginning I helped run Blyth Hearts F.C. which played a number of friendly matches with other clubs running at the time – the Cowpen & Crofton, Top House pub, Blyth AA (a tongue in the cheek Alchoholic's Anonymous), Blyth Academicals, Tyne Tees Television and Blyth Police

After a while four of us who were running teams – Len Hayward, Jimmy Hopkins, Alfie Parks and myself – called a meeting in the British Legion club in Waterloo Road which later became the Blyth Labour Club and is now the Flying Horse pub. We decided to form a competition and that was how the Blyth and District Sunday League came into existence in 1960.

It was completely unofficial with clubs themselves providing the referees and that was how I took up the whistle. Many an argument broke out particularly if you were refereeing your own side – not just from the opposition but your own players also had plenty of grumbles. I think some of the grumbles subsided after I passed the referee's examination and eventually spent 25 years in the middle taking charge of matches in the Northern Alliance and Miners' Welfare League.

Finding pitches in the early days of our league was no problem at all as thanks to the support of Blyth council and particularly Ken Earnshaw who was in charge of the parks in the borough. We had three at Cowpen, two at Gloucester Lodge, and one each at Broadway, Eleventh Avenue and Seaton Sluice.

After serving as chairman for two years I took over as secretary of the league which then had twenty four teams in two divisions. It was a job I was to hold for seventeen years.

In 1963 I had a call from the Northumberland Football Association requesting a meeting in the Kings Head Hotel and the result of that meeting was that we became affiliated to the FA. It also meant we could tap into the Referees' Pool providing us with official and qualified referees for our games. One of them who became a regular man in the middle at our matches was Jimmy Marnock, a policeman in Blyth,

Alan and his trophies.

whose services after his death were recognized by the establishment of the J.D. Marnock Cup competition. Others were George Cook, who lived in Newsham, Alan Hetherington, who later refereed in the Football League and Dennis Fowler.

The league just went from strength to strength. Wilkinsons Sword Edge at Cramlington gave us the F.A. Randolph Cup, named after a director of the company,

Alan Davison refereed when the Whistle Cup was contested at Croft Park, the home of Blyth Spartans, between teams from the North and South Blyth British Rail depots captained by Kenny Ryder (South Blyth), left, and Bill Harland. The cup got its name from the fact it was made out of a railway engine whistle.

and we eventually found ourselves with three divisions of the league which had been boosted by sides joining from Ashington, Newbiggin, Morpeth and Cramlington.

Some time later I was approached by Derek Raffle, a Blyth councillor, who lived in Hartford and ran one of the teams there. He asked if we would have any objection if the Cramlington sides broke away to start their own league. My reply was the more the merrier which rather surprised him as he would be taking some of our teams away. But the formation of the Cramlington and District Sunday League meant other teams in that part of the Valley came into being. Our whole intention of launching our league was the development of the sport in East Northumberland, something which I think we have successfully achieved.

In 1982 I was honoured to receive a life membership of the league and was the guest of honour at the 50th anniversary of the founding of the league held in the Newsham and New Delaval Social Club.

Blyth Hearts Juvenile Jazz Band

Running the league was a time consuming job but I was even more busy with the Blyth Hearts Juvenile Jazz Band. My involvement came about when my three young daughters, Sylvia, Susan and Sharon, asked permission from me and my wife Sylvia to join a juvenile jazz band at the Isabella Colliery.

We discovered that Eddie and Betty Madison were running the Blyth Marines, a collection of youngsters trained in marching to the sound of kazoos. Eddie was the trainer and Betty the secretary and Sylvia and I soon became involved.

In 1981 my wife and I decided to form the Blyth Hearts. We started with seven youngsters but within a month, by word of mouth, we had twenty eight in the band. At that time the noise they made with their kazoos was not exactly music to the ears but we were able to get across to them that by pitching your voice like a singer a far better noise could be made.

For twelve months all we did was train and raise money to buy uniforms and instruments and eventually in 1982 took part in our first competition at Dipton in County Durham. We cleared the board winning the parade, display, music and drum sections. That was the start of a huge collection of trophies numbering at its peak over 400 – all of them in my house at some time. Fortunately half of them had to be sent back after a year.

Alan and his late wife, Sylvia.

Our transport to the competitions all over the country was in a coach we bought for £1,000 from a company in Tow Law. It was about thirty years old but the company painted it for us even putting the name of the band on the side. It cost £500 to insure and did ten to twelve miles to the gallon.

We were fortunate when the late Jean Bell, manageress of the Keel Row Shopping Mall, sponsored us to the tune of £500 a year for several years which helped defray the costs. Unfortunately change of ownership of the Mall lost us that income.

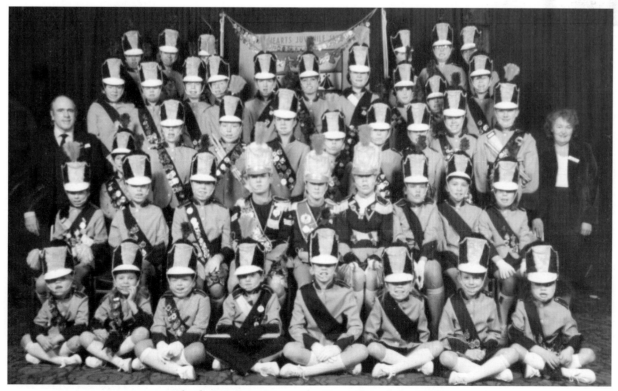

Blyth Hearts Juvenile Jazz Band in 1982.

Since then we have still raised enough cash to have a further three buses. Because, of course, we couldn't afford a new vehicle they weren't all that reliable and we have been stranded on a number of occasions particularly on the M6. This meant emergency rescues by parents and supporters driving from Blyth. On one occasion, on the M6, the bus broke down and it cost £1,000 to get it back to Blyth. First we had to get it towed to a garage in a little village off the motorway then I had to travel back to Blyth in one of the rescue mini-buses, collect our fitter, Craig Wilson, buy the part, a clutch, that was needed, and return to Cumbria where it took Craig and I a whole day to fit it.

Juvenile Jazz bands have come on a lot since they were set up in the 1970's. There are still kazoos on display but also drums, glockenspiels, marimbas and xylophones. Reckoning up the other day I discovered that since we formed the Blyth Hearts thirty years ago 745 youngsters have been involved, some of the more recent recruits being children of original members. More than 70,000 road miles have been covered – all driven by me. The band has been second twice, two years running, in the World Championships held in Liverpool where we were against forty bands. The big event of the year though is the annual Jazz Band Jamboree held at various venues in England and Scotland each October. Almost every jazz band in Britain turns out for what is a marvellous occasion.

People ask me the purpose of juvenile jazz bands and I tell them because it instils discipline, self-respect and motivation. Not bad motives.

Epilogue

Alan Davison closes these memories of Blyth and I am delighted we have managed to commit many fascinating reminiscences into print before they are lost forever. It is a sad fact that photographs and interesting and historically valuable documents regularly find themselves cast into the recycling blue bins by relatives who don't understand their importance. If it was not for the great work of Bob Balmer and Gordon Smith, the leading Blyth historians, and earlier the late Bill Sullivan, the heritage of the town would be the poorer by far.

Also to be given full credit are the early Blyth historians who helped found the local History Society, all sadly passed on: Bill Dawson, headmaster of Bebside School, Bob Morley who taught at the Bebside School, Jim Scott, a teacher at Newlands and Syd Soulsby headmaster New Delaval School. Syd was a also a gifted photographer and Gordon has many of his colour slides taken in Blyth in the 1950s to 1960s.

The author in Australia with boa constrictor (Oh dear, it's still found its way in the book see page 5 – Publisher).

As far as loss of parts of our heritage is concerned the takeover of the Blyth News by another national newspaper group is a case in point. The office in Regent Street was being refurbished and all the film negatives taken by the late Ray Dunn, a photographer on the paper for many years who was meticulous in his filing, were being cast into a skip. Bob Balmer was tipped off by Ray and rescued them literally out of the bin. They have now been committed to the computer by Gordon Smith to live forever.

The interest in this book even before it went on sale led to me thinking of writing a Part Two and it is amazing when you put your thinking cap on just how many individuals in Blyth have stories to tell about themselves and companies and organisations they have worked for. I look forward to it.

Jim Harland